MW01004673

"*Growing in Gratit*
doubted, suffere_
the Garden of Eden and continuing throughout the whole
span of Scripture, Mary K. Mohler invites us to embrace the
'big-dealness' of gratitude for those who know Christ. In
straightforward yet deeply penetrating ways, Mary opens the
theological doorway to a grateful heart as graciously as she
has opened the door of her home to thousands throughout
her years of ministry. With perceptive illustrations, she
skillfully wins us over until we are 'abounding in thanksgiving'
(Colossians 2:7) in happy obedience to God's word. This
book would be a treasure if only for the truth found in her
list of 'Ten ways to thank the Lord when it hurts.' But read
the whole thing! Both your head and your heart will be lifted
up into new paths of gratitude."

Jani Ortlund, *Executive Vice President, Renewal Ministries*

"Popular mottos and self-help advice on being thankful
abound. But Mary K. Mohler takes us deeper to explore the
theological root of gratitude and the hindrances that keep us
from developing a truly grateful heart. In this book, you'll
find solid, effective counsel. So listen up! I'm confident you'll
be grateful you did."

Mary A. Kassian, *author of Girls Gone Wise*

"It was a real joy to listen to Mary's wisdom from years of
learning thankfulness. I love how she encourages us to stop and
pray, putting into action what we're learning, and her chapters
on hindrances to gratitude are fresh and insightful. I have been
challenged by Mary's shrewd observations and genuinely can
say this book has helped me to be growing in gratitude."

Linda Allcock, *London Women's Convention*

"Mary K. Mohler bares her lovely and redeemed heart in this book. And as I read it, I found myself scribbling notes, making book lists from Mary's recommendations, and stopping to pray in both repentance and thanksgiving. I did this because I want the habits and heart of this book to seep into my own. Simple but not simplistic, profound but not inaccessible, this book shows how Christian gratitude, more than list-making and positive thinking, nourishes believers to become more like our Savior, preparing us to be conduits for his grace. As I was reading this book, I felt as if I was sitting with Mary in her kitchen, listening, learning, praying, and thanking God for the unity and beauty and power of the gospel to equip us, truly, to every good work, including the good work of thanking him when agonizing circumstances do not change. Although it was written for women, all Christians will benefit from this book."

Rosaria Butterfield, *author of The Secret Thoughts of an Unlikely Convert; and Openness Unhindered*

"Gratitude is a lost art in our entitled and consumeristic society. Even in the church we have lost a sense of thankfulness for not only what we have but also for all that God has done for us in Christ. Mary K. Mohler exhorts us to fight that tendency, and she does so with care and with insight. I was convicted and encouraged to not only grow in my gratitude toward the Lord but also to pass on this legacy to my children. This book is a gift to God's people, who must learn to not forget all his benefits."

Courtney Reissig, *author of Glory in the Ordinary; and The Accidental Feminist*

"Gratitude isn't an autumn attitude. As Mary K. Mohler explains, it is a deeply theological emotion that shapes and reveals our heart for God in every season of life. We are grateful to God for this insightful book that helps us all to see the gravity and the grace of gratitude."

Carolyn Mahaney and Nicole Whitacre,
authors of True Beauty; and True Feelings

"*Growing in Gratitude* by Mary K. Mohler is an informative and inspiring volume on what has become a vanishing virtue for this 'entitled' generation. Mohler reminds us that the movement from grace to gratitude to giving is a divine mandate worthy of our most diligent efforts even in the midst of personal challenges and suffering. Even as your 'thorn list' runs parallel to your 'praise list,' you must choose to focus on the Lord and his power and love more than on your own pain and difficulty!"

Dorothy Kelley Patterson, *Professor of Theology in Women's Studies, Southwestern Baptist Theological Seminary*

"Entitlement is the death of gratitude, and so no wonder our age is awash in unthankfulness. By contrast, the Christian life is a life of gratitude (how could it be otherwise when we are saved by God's grace alone!), but being thankful is easier said than done 'through all the changing scenes of life, in trouble and in woe.' Mary Mohler addresses this vital subject here, positively helping us grow in gratitude as she points us to God's word. I'm thankful for Mary, and I'm thankful for her study of Bible-based, grace-empowered thankfulness in this book, *Growing in Gratitude*, and her encouragement of us in it!"

Ligon Duncan, *Chancellor and CEO, Reformed Theological Seminary*

"With penetrating insight, Mary K. Mohler provides a thoughtful and thorough study of biblical gratitude and the necessity for each of us to grow in this area. She speaks with conviction and clarity, with humility and humor. I strongly recommend this Scripture-saturated, theologically robust, and eminently practical book."

Jodi Ware, *wife, mother, grandmother, and faculty member of the Seminary Wives Institute at the Southern Baptist Theological Seminary*

Mary K. Mohler

Growing in Gratitude

thegoodbook
COMPANY

To R. Albert Mohler, Jr.
The love of my life, whose amazing wisdom makes
writing books look easy, and whose love and leadership
fill my life with joy and gratitude.

Growing in Gratitude
© Mary K. Mohler/The Good Book Company, 2018

Published by:
The Good Book Company
Tel (US): 866 244 2165
Tel (UK): 0333 123 0880
Email (US): info@thegoodbook.com
Email (UK): info@thegoodbook.co.uk

Websites:
North America: www.thegoodbook.com
UK: www.thegoodbook.co.uk
Australia: www.thegoodbook.com.au
New Zealand: www.thegoodbook.co.nz

Unless otherwise indicated, Scripture quotations are from The Holy Bible, English Standard Version (ESV), copyright © 2001 by Crossway, a publishing ministry of Good News Publishers. Used by permission.

ISBN: 9781784982331 | Printed in the UK

Design by André Parker

Contents

Introduction:
A Life of Thankfulness

The sight is glorious as the leaves are changing in Kentucky. The temperature is dropping and most of us are glad to pull out vests, sweaters, and jackets that have been stashed away since April. The smell of pumpkin-spiced everything seems to be everywhere. Yes, Thanksgiving is just ten days from now.

So, it's time to think about being thankful yet again. We have meal planning to do and travel arrangements to make—and the Christmas shopping season has somehow managed to leapfrog over Thanksgiving. Yet we will not skip over this much-celebrated American holiday that comes just one month before Christmas. Challenged by a glut of blog posts and articles about thankfulness that floods our inboxes every November, we will slow down long enough to be thankful. It's what we do.

Those around us who don't follow Christ will enjoy the four-day weekend as they too gather with friends and family to express gratitude to one another—and perhaps to thank Mother Nature for the change of weather and the Man Upstairs for letting them live another year free of disaster.

But we, as believers in the Lord Jesus Christ, can do much more than that. We are profoundly grateful to our Creator for creating, loving, saving, and sustaining us to the praise of his great glory. So, for us, Thanksgiving Day is just like every other day in terms of our deep gratitude, although we probably take more time to be mindful of it as we pause before a meal of turkey, dressing, and pumpkin pie.

Or do we?

Is it possible that we daily intend to be grateful but fall short of it becoming second nature to us? Every single breath we draw is a gift from our Almighty God. That simple and profound truth is too often lost on us. We are surrounded by a contemporary culture where *entitlement* rules. People are convinced they deserve to be happy, healthy, rich, and empowered. Self-absorption creeps in and takes root.

Most of us know better. And we know we should do a better job of remembering this. So why do we need a whole book to remind us about what we already know? *Be more thankful. Got it. Now on to deeper subjects...*

But wait! This book is not just meant to inspire you to grow in gratitude. Please keep reading! Gratitude is a rich theological issue. The presence or absence of it in our lives is very telling. It truly is a big deal. I am not talking about a "count your many blessings, name them one by one" kind of gratitude to God. I am talking about a deep sense of awe ingrained in our minds. I am talking about an awareness, in every waking moment, of the glorious truth that the God of the universe is infinite in all of his perfections. And he *loves* us.

Scripture is full of commands for us to praise and give thanks to our Lord, so it really does matter. What a delight it should be for us to thank him. My hope for this book is to encourage you to embrace the life-changing virtue of gratitude, and to let it spill out into everything you say and do. Perhaps you remember a time, when you first came to faith in Christ, when you had boundless joy and a grateful heart. What happened to diminish that? Let's think about ways to re-discover that joy.

I have learned so much as I have explored what true gratitude is, and I am eager to share it with you. I have realized that, even as redeemed sinners, we face common hindrances to gratitude, so let's tackle those head on and look to God's word to find clear strategies to combat them. You will also be heartened to read true stories from people who can praise God for the victories he has given them over some of these hindrances.

As we focus on gratitude in this book, may we be drawn closer to the Lord as we invite the Holy Spirit to convict us through biblical truth. May we be encouraged by those who have gone before, as their writings give us much to consider. May we seek to embrace gratitude in new and practical ways. May we be women who leave a legacy of thankfulness that others wish to follow. May we praise the Lord with our whole hearts.

An Overflowing Fountain

Gratitude. Thankfulness. Praise to our great God. None of us has ever come close to living the life of a consistently grateful believer. We may strive to do so. But, as with most New Year's resolutions, even if we aim for a more consistent Bible-reading plan, a specific prayer list, and intentional expressions of gratitude, we easily get sidelined by our own lack of discipline.

Why is that? Why do we find consistent gratitude to God so hard? Are we making this too complicated?

Back to the Basics

We know we are supposed to count our blessings from the Lord—and write nice thank-you notes! Scripture is filled with commands for us to be thankful, be filled with gratitude, have grateful hearts, abound with thanksgiving, and more. Believers in the Lord Jesus Christ are to be characterized by gratitude.

Let's remind ourselves of the wonderful gifts believers have in Christ and will want to thank the Lord for. We were once hopelessly separated from God. We had no way to save ourselves from hell, no matter how hard we tried nor how many good things we did. But we were justified the moment we were prompted by the Holy Spirit to confess our sin to God the Father and believe that Jesus Christ alone stands in our place as our perfect substitute. From that moment on, God the Father has looked at us through the sacrificial death and resurrection of Jesus Christ, and is satisfied that our sin debt was paid in full through the shed blood of Christ. The Holy Spirit now lives in us forever. That process is how we stand forgiven and clothed in Christ's righteousness! Wonderful! (You will find some of the wonderful gifts believers have "in Christ" in 2 Timothy 1:9; Ephesians 1:4, 7, 11-14; 2:11-13; Romans 8:38-39; 2 Corinthians 5:17, 21; and Galatians 3:26.)

As Christians, these glorious truths shape how we want to live. We spend the rest of our lives seeking to be more like Christ while still sinners on this earth. We live our lives in gratitude for what Christ has done for us—and we seek to be more like him even though we still sin. We look forward to the time when we will live with the Lord in heaven forever in our glorified bodies and will sin no more.

What an unspeakable gift we have been given through the perfect sacrifice of God's own Son, Jesus Christ. Hence, every single Christian should be filled with gratitude. No matter what our age, race, culture, language, social status, or life circumstances, all Christians should be known as characteristically grateful people. We, above all humans, have overwhelming cause to be thankful.

Grateful or Grumpy?

Wouldn't it be wonderful if gratitude was one of the first things that comes to mind when people think about believers in Jesus Christ? They may not agree with us—and may even pity us for what they perceive to be our wasted lives—but even so, the world should be struck by how grateful we are for the gifts we wholeheartedly believe we possess from God alone.

Are they? Or do they too often see us as complainers or moody types who are frustrated and fraught with worry, just as they are?

Let's state the obvious: more than anything else, we are the most thankful for the inexpressible gift of grace in the salvation that we have in Christ alone. Paul reminds us at the beginning of Ephesians 2 just how desperately lost every single one of us was until God intervened (Ephesians 2:1-3). We were all once separated from God and totally unable to save ourselves— we were hopeless and helpless without Christ.

But Ephesians 2 continues with that dazzling—arguably the greatest—two-word theological phrase: *but God.*

> *But God, being rich in mercy, because of the great
> love with which he loved us, even when we were dead in
> our trespasses, made us alive together with Christ—
> by grace you have been saved—and raised us up with
> him and seated us with him in the heavenly places
> in Christ Jesus, so that in the coming ages he might
> show the immeasurable riches of his grace in kindness
> toward us in Christ Jesus.*   EPHESIANS 2:4-7

What a stark contrast in what we read before and after the words "but God." Once, we were separated from God and unable to save ourselves—but as believers, we are saved to the uttermost. We did not earn or deserve this gift and we cannot lose it—this is such good news since we know that if we could lose it, we would! We do not do good works in order to cause our salvation or retain it, but we do them as a *result* of it and in *gratitude* for it.

The Bible Is So Clear About Gratitude

From cover to cover, the precious word of God confronts us with passage after passage related to praise and thanksgiving. Let's look at some specific passages.

Paul encourages us earnestly many times in his inspired writings to be thankful. One such text is found in Colossians:

> *Therefore, as you received Christ Jesus the Lord,
> so walk in him, rooted and built up in him and*

established in the faith, just as you were taught,
abounding in thanksgiving. COLOSSIANS 2:6-7

The Greek word used here for "abounding" means "overflowing"—and it is a *continuous* action. It is the result of being rooted, built up, and established. We are to be like a fountain that is continually filled to overflowing. We are not only to exhibit gratitude but we are to overflow with it, such that it spills out into all that we do.

This is not talking about a count-your-blessings-and-squirrel-them-away-in-a-pretty-notebook type of gratitude. Nor is it a suggestion to be a glass-half-full type of happy-clappy Christian in the midst of disaster. This gratitude is so much more than that. It is transformational. It is an intentional mindset that stems from the fact that since we have indeed received Christ Jesus the Lord, are walking with him, and are rooted and established in the faith, we will overflow with thanksgiving as a result. In spite of how we fall short of the glory of God in our sinful natures on this earth, we are blessed with a glimpse into what a phenomenal gift we have been given in Christ. We will want to overflow with praise and thanksgiving as a result.

Think about that picture of the overflowing fountain. If you should happen to jostle us, we spill gratitude. You don't have to reach way down into our psyches or personalities to discover that, okay, Christians are indeed thankful people. You should not have to ask us the right questions to eventually get there. No! Gratitude abounds, overflows, flows out as a characteristic of who we are—on good days and bad ones too.

Grace Leads to Gratitude

You cannot push a button and make gratitude start to gush. It comes as a result of receiving Christ Jesus as Lord. The grace we have received compels us to be grateful, and in turn to desire to show grace and generosity to others.

Here is another way to look at how gratitude is vital and fulfills such a key role in the life of the believer. Think of it as the middle step in a three-step process.

Grace — Gratitude — Giving Generously

Paul says in Colossians 2 that we have received Christ Jesus as Lord and should walk in him. This is all about grace. We have received this free gift of grace and our response is thanksgiving—but it does not end there. Our thankful hearts spur us on to act like grateful people who in turn seek to show appreciation in a variety of ways to build up the church and spread the gospel.

We do not stall on the fact that we have new life in Christ; instead it spurs us on to live a life of gratitude that in turn causes us to be generous people. We will want to be generous with our time, talents, and treasures. Grace leads to gratitude which leads to giving— and the Lord is glorified in the process. Fabulous!

Paul reminds us of that end result in 2 Corinthians:

For it is all for your sake, so that as grace extends to more and more people it may increase thanksgiving, to the glory of God. 2 CORINTHIANS 4:15

Returning to Paul's epistle to the church at Colossae, we see that he urges his readers three times in one short passage to be thankful. Do we get the idea that this is beyond important?

*And let the peace of Christ rule in your hearts, to which indeed you were called in one body. And **be thankful**. Let the word of Christ dwell in you richly, teaching and admonishing one another in all wisdom, singing psalms and hymns and spiritual songs, **with thankfulness** in your hearts to God. And whatever you do, in word or deed, do everything in the name of the Lord Jesus, **giving thanks** to God the Father through him.*

COLOSSIANS 3:15-17 *(bold text mine)*

What a privilege to seek not only to have the peace of Christ rule in our hearts but to have those same hearts be thankful. Gratitude is so much more than running through the same old lists in our heads as rushed prayers while nodding off at night. We must not trivialize it for the simple reason that the Bible does not do so. Paul is here describing characteristically thankful people. And surely we want to be such people.

The writer of the book of Hebrews provides yet another prompt in chapter 12:

> *Therefore let us be grateful for receiving a kingdom*
> *that cannot be shaken, and thus let us offer to God*
> *acceptable worship, with reverence and awe.*
>
> HEBREWS 12:28

Grateful Sheep

Let's also look to the well-known words of the 100th psalm as a classic example of a call to gratitude:

> *Know that the LORD, he is God!*
> *It is he who made us, and we are his;*
> *we are his people, and the sheep of his pasture.*
>
> *Enter his gates with thanksgiving,*
> *and his courts with praise!*
> *Give thanks to him; bless his name!*   PSALM 100:3-4

Here's another great visual for us to embrace. We are now his sheep and belong to him forever. So it follows that we enter his gates with thanksgiving and praise as we bless his name. Further, we dwell safely within those gates under our loving Shepherd's providential care.

Consider Isaiah 43:25. Neither praise nor thanksgiving is mentioned, but these words should cause every believer to stand in awe:

I, I am he who blots out your transgressions for my
own sake, and I will not remember your sins.

ISAIAH 43:25

Our all-knowing God keeps no record of our sins for the sake of his great glory. As believers, we stand before him clothed in the righteousness of Christ. The Lord has not only blotted out our sins but he will remember them no more. Our gratitude should thus know no bounds.

The Opposite of Gratitude Spells Disaster

By contrast, let's think about the opposite of this virtue. We can better understand gratitude by looking at ingratitude. We can trace ingratitude all the way back to Eden.

Now the serpent was more crafty than any other beast
of the field that the LORD God had made.

He said to the woman, "Did God actually say, 'You
shall not eat of any tree in the garden'?" And the
woman said to the serpent, "We may eat of the fruit
of the trees in the garden, but God said, 'You shall
not eat of the fruit of the tree that is in the midst of
the garden, neither shall you touch it, lest you die.'"
But the serpent said to the woman, "You will not
surely die. For God knows that when you eat of it
your eyes will be opened, and you will be like God,
knowing good and evil." So when the woman saw that
the tree was good for food, and that it was a delight to

21

*the eyes, and that the tree was to be desired to make
one wise, she took of its fruit and ate, and she also
gave some to her husband who was with her, and
he ate. Then the eyes of both were opened, and they
knew that they were naked. And they sewed fig leaves
together and made themselves loincloths.*

GENESIS 3:1-7

Picture the idyllic lives of Adam and Eve in the paradise of Eden. All was perfect and unblemished. Every need was supplied in that place of utter joy, beauty, and contentment. God said they could eat of all but one tree. But being given all of the other trees was not good enough for them. Oh, if only they had just been grateful for what was given to them instead of wanting more. Ingratitude is thus at the root of the original sin in the garden—resulting in the fall.

Paul, as inspired by the Holy Spirit, states in Romans 1:18, "For the wrath of God is revealed from heaven against all ungodliness and unrighteousness of men," and goes on to state three times how God "gave them up," (v 24, 26, 28)—perhaps the most terrifying phrase in all of Scripture. He gave them up for two simple reasons:

*For although they knew God, **they did not honor
him as God or give thanks to him,** but they
became futile in their thinking, and their foolish hearts
were darkened. Claiming to be wise, they became fools,
and exchanged the glory of the immortal God for*

*images resembling mortal man and birds and animals
and creeping things.*

ROMANS 1:21-23 *(bold text mine)*

They neither honored God nor gave him thanks. Simple yet profound. It is striking that these flaws are of so much consequence that they trigger such a strong response from God. Did you notice that these flaws are not related to complex issues requiring lots of words and deep discussion? The issues were failing to honor God and to show him gratitude. The people decided it was more important for themselves to be happy and wise in their own eyes. They foolishly did what they thought was best even though it robbed God of his glory. Their actions had the disastrous and unthinkable result of their being abandoned by God!

Paul later includes ingratitude in a list of traits in 2 Timothy 3 that will characterize godlessness in the last days before Jesus returns:

*But understand this, that in the last days there will
come times of difficulty. For people will be lovers
of self, lovers of money, proud, arrogant, abusive,
disobedient to their parents, **ungrateful,** unholy,
heartless, unappeasable, slanderous, without self-
control, brutal, not loving good, treacherous, reckless,
swollen with conceit, lovers of pleasure rather than
lovers of God, having the appearance of godliness, but
denying its power. Avoid such people.*

2 TIMOTHY 3:1-5 *(bold text mine)*

Look at all of those descriptors. And right in the middle of this list of wretched traits, we find the characteristic of being *ungrateful*. Paul is clear that ingratitude is not a trivial issue but is among the sins that plunge depraved sinners further and further away from the Lord.

Ungrateful Grumblers

We learn so many lessons about what not to do as we study the grumbling and rebellious Israelites. Exodus 16 gives a good snapshot of their ingratitude:

> *And the people of Israel said to [Moses and Aaron],*
> *"Would that we had died by the hand of the* Lord
> *in the land of Egypt, when we sat by the meat pots*
> *and ate bread to the full, for you have brought us out*
> *into this wilderness to kill this whole assembly with*
> *hunger."*   Exodus 16:3

What stunningly short memories these people had. The Lord had miraculously delivered them from the hands of the Egyptians. We read just fourteen chapters earlier in Exodus 2:

> *During those many days the king of Egypt died,*
> *and the people of Israel groaned because of their*
> *slavery and cried out for help. Their cry for rescue*
> *from slavery came up to God. And God heard their*
> *groaning, and God remembered his covenant with*

> *Abraham, with Isaac, and with Jacob. God saw the*
> *people of Israel—and **God knew**.*
>
> > EXODUS 2:23-25 *(bold text mine)*

God *knew* all right. His steadfast love for his chosen people was unfailing, but their short memories gave way to their deceitful hearts. Exodus 16 continues with the account: not only manna but quail was provided from heaven to meet their needs perfectly. What must it have been like when that manna began to fall and those quail arrived like instant dinner on a plate? No traps were needed, for quail are ground-dwelling birds which sit motionless if alarmed. These birds could be caught by hand!

Did the Israelites feel foolish and ashamed for doubting the Lord's provision and perfect plan? Apparently not in any long-standing way, since we read of this pattern being repeated over and over and over again. Sadly, we are often just like the Israelites, as ingratitude becomes our default response instead of a rare occurrence. The profound plea of the psalmist in Psalm 90 is one that I often pray as I fight my own tendency toward ingratitude:

> *Satisfy us in the morning with your steadfast love,*
> *that we may rejoice and be glad all our days.*
>
> > PSALM 90:14

Looking Ahead

My favorite cultural commentator of the age is none other than my beloved husband, Albert Mohler, who said this on his website:

*We need to recognize that gratitude is a deeply
theological act when it's rightly understood. As
a matter of fact, thankfulness is a theology in
microcosm. You come to understand an entire system
of theology, an entire set of doctrines and beliefs, by
what the Christian believes about gratitude and this
is thus the key to understanding what we really believe
about God, what we really believe about ourselves,
what we really believe about the world we experience.*[1]

Clearly, this topic is worthy of our attention and should be a hallmark of our lives.

Precious Father,

*As we consider how to grow in gratitude, remind
us of how we were once overwhelmed with joy at the
unspeakably wonderful gift of your kindness to us in
Christ Jesus.*

*May we rediscover that joy that has waned.
May we resolve to keep it in the forefront of our
minds as we press forward to the day when we will see
our Savior's face.*

Make us grateful people for your glory alone!

In Jesus' name,

Amen.

Think It Through

1. Is it a stretch to think of yourself as one who, when bumped, spills out gratitude? How can this word-picture help you to be more intentional about living out thankfulness?

2. Can you see clear examples in your own life of how grace leads to gratitude—and gratitude leads to generosity? How does remembering what the Lord has done for you motivate you to serve others?

The Gratitude Twins

Have you ever noticed that when a favorable biopsy report is received, or the blue lights seen in the rear-view mirror turn out to be for someone else, or the treasured smartphone is finally located under the couch, there is an almost universal knee-jerk response? "Thank God!"

It pops out of the mouths of even the most nominal believer in a higher power. Some may say it just in case there really is a God and he happens to be listening. Sadly, for many, that will be the only thought or mention of God—let alone any gratitude toward him—until the next time disaster is averted.

But Christians are different. "Thank God" is not merely something we blurt out in relief but also the mindset with which we want to conduct our lives on this earth. We confidently believe there is one true God—and he is indeed listening.

Two Levels of Gratitude

Wise believers from centuries past have studied what Scripture says about gratitude. The fruit of their labors can be very helpful to us.

One in particular is Jonathan Edwards, the great early-American theologian and pastor who lived to be just 54 years old. He died in 1758 as the result of an experimental smallpox inoculation, leaving his wife and eleven children. In his rather short and very difficult life, Edwards was used by the Lord to preach, teach, model, and write about significant biblical concepts that are still impacting his readers today.

Edwards described two levels of gratitude. I find his classification very helpful as we consider what gratitude means for the believer in Christ. In his work *Religious Affections* he said this:

> *Gratitude is one of the natural affections of the soul of man ... Gratitude is an affection one has toward another, for loving him, or gratifying him ... There is doubtless such a thing as a gracious gratitude, which does greatly differ from all that gratitude which natural men experience. It differs in the following respects:*

> *True gratitude or thankfulness to God for his kindness to us, arises from a foundation laid before,*

> *of love to God for what he is in himself ... In a*
> *gracious gratitude, men are affected with ... that*
> *wonderful and unparalleled grace of God, which is*
> *manifested in the work of redemption, and shines*
> *forth in the face of Jesus Christ.*[2]

Unpacking Edwards' Marvelous Work

Edwards describes two levels of gratitude:

1. **Natural gratitude.** This is thankfulness for blessings received—for good gifts.
2. **Gracious gratitude.** This is thankfulness for God himself—for who he is.

We rightly show gratitude to God when we thank him for his blessings to us, which are undeserved and so greatly appreciated. We do count our blessings— this is that **natural gratitude** to which Edwards refers, and it is suggested for believers in several places in the Bible (for example, Ephesians 5:20; 1 Thessalonians 5:18; James 1:17).

Yet Edwards' point is that when we offer thanks to the Lord, it is often solely due to his gifts to us. There is nothing that goes before it nor underlies it. There is thus no foundation for what he calls this natural gratitude.

But the other form is different. **Gracious gratitude** is primary and is a deeper form of gratitude that thanks God for *who he is*. Gracious gratitude takes no notice of gifts received but focuses on praising the Giver for his character and his incomparable love. This type of gratitude reflects the fact that we have a relationship with the one true and living God. He is not an abstract being out there somewhere. He is God, and we have the unspeakable privilege of praising him just for being God, whatever our circumstances—whether we are at the top of our game or down and out.

Gracious Gratitude Reflects the Heart

Gracious gratitude should spring up as a flowing fountain as we are ever mindful of God's character. Gratitude of this kind for the attributes of God shows that the Holy Spirit is truly at work in our hearts. It is a defining characteristic of a Christian, since while unbelievers may thank God for his gifts, only Christians thank God for his holiness.

Are you ever bothered by doubts about the security of your salvation? If so, ask yourself whether you are thankful for God himself, rather than only for what he can give you. If you are, you can take great comfort in realizing that your genuine gracious gratitude—your thankfulness for who God is—is a marvelous result of the fact that you are forever safe in the care of your personal Savior, who died and rose again for you. How kind of the Lord to allow our gratitude to him to also serve as assurance to us!

While both natural and gracious gratitude are found in the life of a follower of Christ, one is secondary, and the other primary. But both are needed. Dr. John Piper is helpful in explaining this further:

God is not glorified if the foundation of our gratitude is the worth of the gift and not the excellency of the Giver. If gratitude is not rooted in the beauty of God before the gift, it is probably disguised idolatry. May God grant us a heart to delight in him for who he is so that all our gratitude for his gifts will be the echo of our joy in the excellency of the Giver![3]

Have you ever thought of gratitude as idolatry? It certainly can be if we are more thrilled with the blessings God has given to us than we are thrilled by the fact that we serve the infinite, eternal, all-powerful, all-knowing, loving God. That puts things in a whole different perspective.

Misplaced Affection

Imagine a young man nervously rehearsing the words in his mind over and over again. He has to get this right. He sincerely wants to be articulate and profound when he asks his beloved girlfriend to be his fiancée. The setting has been carefully orchestrated and the ring is safely in its box in his pocket. The moment arrives. He is pleased by how he is able to profess his love for her in spite of his anxiety. He opens the box and asks the question. She is overcome with joy, but after a quick embrace, she simply cannot stop looking at and gushing about the beautiful ring.

He is glad she approves. That's a relief as it cost him a great deal. He is sure she will get over the newness of this beautiful gem on her finger but she does not. He is eager to hear words of affirmation from her besides the simple "yes" that she gave to his question about marriage. He is expecting to hear her express her deep love for him, using words that he will remember for a lifetime. But those words do not come. She just cannot stop gushing about the qualities of the ring. From its sparkle, size, shape, setting, cut, and clarity, to its perfect fit, she is enthralled.

As the hours and then days pass, the newness of the sight of that ring on her finger does not fade. He becomes completely perplexed, as she seems to be obsessed with the ring itself and has little or no affection, affirmation, or words of appreciation for the giver of the ring, except to thank him for purchasing it for her.

What a bizarre story! That man should request the ring back and run, right? Who wants to be married to someone who merely wants a mate with exquisite taste in gifts?

Making Gracious Gratitude Primary

But is that not how we treat the Lord at times? We approach him with *natural gratitude* for the multiple gifts he has given, but we fail to be first and foremost grateful for who he is and the fact that we can know him. When we fail to lead with *gracious gratitude*, we act just like that fiancée who has misplaced her affections onto the gift and ignored the giver.

To take this a step further, we don't deserve anything favorable from the Lord, but instead deserve condemnation. Our primary gracious gratitude acknowledges this and does not move on too quickly from there. How often do we take time to meditate on the nature of the one true God in heaven? Among so many other things:

- He holds all power and authority.
- He knows everything and can be everywhere at once.
- He is self-created.
- He has no beginning and no end.
- He never changes.
- And he has made a way for us to know him through Jesus Christ.

Does that make your heart sing? Why not stop reading right now and thank God for each of these wonderful truths about him.

The Overflowing Glory of the Lord

We will want to express our gratitude to the Lord for who he is every day of our lives. Never get over the wonder of what little our feeble minds can understand about our unsearchable God. Praise him for his nature using the most profound words of thanks that you can. He is not looking for flowery words or eloquent observations. He is looking for sincere awe expressed to him alone from the core of our beings for who he is.

How many times do we read in the Old Testament the words, "Then they will know that I am the Lord"?

God's plan woven through Scripture is to fill the whole earth with the knowledge of his glory alone:

> *For the earth will be filled*
> *with the knowledge of the glory of the LORD*
> *as the waters cover the sea.*
>
> HABAKKUK 2:14

And in the New Testament we see that it is his will that everything that happens will result in the glory of God alone:

> *Oh, the depth of the riches and wisdom and knowledge of God! How unsearchable are his judgments and how inscrutable his ways!*
>
> *"For who has known the mind of the Lord,*
> *or who has been his counselor?"*
> *"Or who has given a gift to him*
> *that he might be repaid?"*
>
> *For from him and through him and to him are all things. To him be glory forever. Amen.*
>
> ROMANS 11:33-36

Gracious Gratitude Should Be What Defines Us

Here is one more quote that further clarifies Jonathan Edwards' work. It is from the late Chuck Colson, founder of Prison Fellowship:

> *This gracious gratitude for who God is also goes to the*
> *heart of who we are in Christ. It is relational, rather*
> *than conditional. Though our world may shatter,*
> *we are secure in him. The fount of our joy, the love*
> *of the God who made us and saved us, cannot be*
> *quenched by any power that exists (Romans 8:28-39).*
> *People who are filled with such radical gratitude are*
> *unstoppable, irrepressible, overflowing with what C.S.*
> *Lewis called "the good infection"—the supernatural,*
> *refreshing love of God that draws others to him.*[4]

Chuck Colson shows us that gracious gratitude is *relational.* We offer it based on the character of our great God and not on the basis of what he has given to us. If every good thing he has given were to vanish, we would still be safe in Christ—and our basis for gracious gratitude would have no reason to be changed at all.

That is certainly easier said than done. However, many of us know Christians who live this out in front of our eyes on a daily basis. They may seem to us to be like a modern-day Job, but they persevere. They continue to faithfully praise our sovereign God no matter what befalls. Oh that we would learn from them and have that "good infection" that C.S. Lewis described.

What a privilege it is for us to discipline our minds to offer gracious gratitude to God for who he is and to glorify his great name. Let's not be so busy thanking God for his gifts that, like the foolish fiancée, we do not primarily thank the Giver. Just do it!

Natural Gratitude

The secondary form, or *natural gratitude* as Edwards called it, is what we are used to thinking of as counting our blessings. It is a genuine, frequent, active appreciation of the Lord for his specific kindnesses and blessings to us. We know it is biblical for us to regularly express it to the Lord.

> *... giving thanks always and for everything to God the Father in the name of our Lord Jesus Christ.*
> EPHESIANS 5:20

But think about this! Natural gratitude on its own merit does not please the Lord. David, the writer of the following psalm, tells us that praising the name of the Lord pleases the Lord more than sacrifices:

> *I will praise the name of God with a song;*
> *I will magnify him with thanksgiving.*
> *This will please the LORD more than an ox*
> *or a bull with horns and hoofs.*   PSALMS 69:30-31

Note that it is the *name* of the Lord that is to be praised here and not his provisions. We must be very careful to give thanks for the Giver of the gifts before we rush on to the gifts themselves. Further, gratitude is an "affection," as Edwards put it. It is a virtue that must be cultivated, and not simply something extra to add to our to-do lists with the notation, "Be more grateful today."

Which Method Works for You?

Many authors recommend starting a blessing journal or a gratitude book in which we can take time daily to list things for which to be grateful. I have even read about campaigns that sound a bit like a weight-loss program where one takes the 30-day challenge to improve in showing gratitude by consistently writing down something daily for a month in hopes of forming a new habit.

Do what works best for you.

I prefer to keep a running list of things for which I am grateful in a small, divided notebook, where I also keep prayer requests and notes from my Bible-reading. My list starts with attributes of God to help me be mindful of gracious gratitude first. What follows is a long and growing list of specific blessings, big and small, for which I am grateful.

I know that there are even "gratitude apps" for our smartphones. Personally, just as I much prefer my hard copy of God's word to study, I am very pleased to have personal aids for spiritual disciplines on paper and in writing—and all in one place. I encourage you to at least try keeping your list in your own writing as this is one task that you may find is more meaningful when not done on a smartphone. But choose whatever works best for you.

It is amazing to look through my prayer-request section and see how God is answering prayer according to his will and his timing, and it is helpful to see how my list of praises expands as I continue my journey on this earth. He is doing marvelous things before our very eyes. How spiritually healthy it is for us all to be specific as we thank the Lord daily for his provisions and gifts. It is natural gratitude that is rooted in Christ.

The Parent Virtue Can Have Many Offspring

As we start to think about hindrances to gratitude in the next few chapters, keep in mind that our topic will allow us to springboard into many areas. I hope you are beginning to see that gratitude is not as simple as it may first appear.

Many centuries ago, the philosopher Cicero made the argument that "gratitude is not only the greatest of virtues, but the parent of all others." If that is true, when we rightly understand gratitude, it can have a cascading effect as it nourishes the growth of other virtues.

- Are you struggling with kindness? Seek ways to be more grateful.
- Do you lose your temper quickly? Work on gratitude.
- Do you wish you could be more patient with others? Cultivate gratitude.

It is the parent of virtues that the Lord can use as a starting point from which so many good character traits may blossom.

Our Father,

Our hearts are full of gracious gratitude for who you are. While we are thankful for all the gifts you give, we are so much more thankful for you, the Giver. We cannot begin to comprehend your infinite nature and boundless love. We stand in awe of you and marvel that we are forever in your care.

Let both gracious and natural gratitude be deeply knit into our hearts.

Let us grow in the parent virtue of gratitude such that our kindness, patience, gentleness, and self-control grow right alongside.

We love you, Lord!

In Jesus' name, Amen.

Think It Through

1. Do you have a blessing journal that works for you? If not, what kind of method could you try so that you will track those things for which you desire to regularly express thanks to the Lord? You may want to start by thanking God for who he is before listing any blessings he has given you.

2. Considering gratitude as a parent virtue, how do you see it nourishing other virtues in your life? Which ones?

Longing For The Lost

I recently stopped by a local store to purchase a frame. I was struck by the beautiful pink and green hues of a framed piece of artwork nearby but as I got closer, I broke out in a huge smile. I knew that the piece was going home with me. Thankfully, it was on sale. It simply says, *Start each day with a grateful heart*. It now hangs behind my desk as I am writing this book.

I need this reminder as much as anyone. I am fairly certain that the artist was not advising us to have a grateful heart because he knew we would meet so many hindrances to doing so. I am not even sure whom the artist had in mind as the recipient of the gratitude. But I am using it as a reminder that thanksgiving to the Lord should be on our minds at the start of each new day no matter what the circumstances.

It is good to give thanks to the LORD,
   to sing praises to your name, O Most High;
   to declare your steadfast love in the morning,
      and your faithfulness by night.   PSALM 92:1-2

As we make daily thankfulness our aim at the start and end of each day, it seems wise to examine some of the hindrances that can affect our gratitude to the Lord so that it's not what it should be. In the next four chapters I intend to look at what I have discovered to be the main hindrances to gratitude, in turn. I will start with the one that I believe is the most serious even though it is likely not the most commonly discussed.

We Rejoice in Our Salvation but Are Burdened for the Lost

One of the marks of believers in Jesus Christ is that we know that our salvation is found in Christ alone. We are ever mindful that there is nothing we did to earn or deserve our status of being forgiven in Christ—but it is nevertheless ours. We joyfully anticipate spending eternity in heaven with Christ, where we will be reunited with all of our fellow believers and will sin no more. Our time here on earth is just a momentary blip compared to the life that is to come.

But we can find that our joyful anticipation is tempered because those who reject Christ will enjoy no such paradise and will be sent to a real place called hell for all eternity (Matthew 10:28;

25:46; 2 Thessalonians 1:9). That is true not just for unrepentant criminals but also for well-meaning neighbors, friends, and family members who do not embrace the gospel. We pray for them earnestly. We look for ways to live out the gospel before their eyes. We seize opportunities to sincerely express the reason for the joy that is within us. As church members, we invest a great deal of money to support missions and evangelism at home and around the world.

But at the end of the day, we are burdened by the fact that our words and actions so often seem to fall on deaf ears. As a result, there is a danger that our own gracious gratitude toward the Lord who saved us is diminished due to our frustration with knowing that our loved ones are not saved.

How are we to respond?

God Alone Sees the Big Picture
For some of us, our struggle with gratitude arises from the rejection of the gospel by those we love.

This sorrow is the same as that which we see Paul experiencing in Romans 9 as he thinks about his Jewish kinsmen:

> *I have great sorrow and unceasing anguish in my heart. For I could wish that I myself were accursed and cut off from Christ for the sake of my brothers, my kinsmen according to the flesh.*
>
> ROMANS 9:2-3

This anguish is right and biblical when we long for non-believers to come to know Christ, but not when we allow it to stop us from showing real gratitude to God.

We find that giving thanks to the Lord is easier when dealing with a personally life-threatening disease than when watching a physically-healthy loved one slam the door on the gospel yet again. As Christians, we can be certain that our life is safely hidden with Christ in God for all eternity (Colossians 3:3) even though we will suffer from disease, injury, and loss. (We will tackle how those issues can hinder our thankful hearts later.) But when our loved ones, though physically healthy, seem to be spiritually dead, it can be overpowering. It can interfere with our gracious gratitude in profound ways. So we need to turn to Scripture and be reminded of what we cannot see:

> *For now we see in a mirror dimly, but then face to face. Now I know in part; then I shall know fully, even as I have been fully known.*
>
> 1 CORINTHIANS 13:12

We see dimly and do not have a deep understanding of what is happening, but even so, we desire to hurry up the results. We want lost people to come to Christ. We struggle to accept that God is at work on his own timetable. The Lord is teaching us yet again that we are simply not in control—and that he alone sees the big picture.

Glorious Stories of Radical Change

I recently heard an amazing and encouraging true story. Two parents had seven children. The father was the only Christian in the family until one of the sons became a believer as well. By the time this father died, still just that one child was a Christian. Everyone else in this large and extended family was lost.

That son was so burdened for his family that he shared the gospel message every way he knew how, but time and time again the message was openly rejected. For some reason, he decided to make an audio recording just in case he died unexpectedly, so that he might have one last chance to make a plea. He told a Christian friend where the recording was located—just in case.

Fast forward a few years: that man died in a plane crash, and the recording was played at his funeral. Five of those siblings and their families, as well as his own wife and children, and even his own mother, were transformed almost immediately after hearing it. Each one made a profession of faith in Christ. Their lives were forever changed and they happily serve the Lord today. Only one brother and his family still reject the gospel. The family continues to pray earnestly for them.

One of the saved brothers is Dr. Miguel Nunez. He and his wife are medical doctors whose lives were turned upside down by Christ. They closed their thriving practices in New York and moved to the Dominican Republic, where Dr. Nunez now serves as pastor of one of the largest evangelical churches in Central America.

Can you imagine what an ecstatically glad reunion there will be in Glory when that earthly family is reunited? I would love to see the reaction of the brother killed in the crash when he hears their stories. How amazed he will be to hear that his brother embraced the gospel, gave up his anticipated medical career, and became a beloved pastor and church planter who now practices medicine on the side!

The first brother sowed seeds and did not live to see them sprout. But in God's perfect timing, they burst forth and continue to bear much fruit! That fruit is above and beyond what he ever dared to ask.

Isn't it amazing how we can, at times, so vastly underestimate God's power? We pray with great earnestness for the salvation of our friends and loved ones. We may hope against hope that maybe at the end of their lives, when faced with the reality of impending death, they will turn to Christ in faith and repentance. As was the case in the Nunez family, God had much bigger plans that would bring glory to his great name alone, even though that faithful brother did not live to see the results.

Seeds May Sprout Later Than We Think

Consider this quote from the nineteenth-century Anglican pastor, Charles Bridges:

> *The seed may lie under the clods till we lie here, and then spring up!*[5]

Isn't that great? What this pastor is saying in old-fashioned English is that the gospel seed we have faithfully planted by sharing our faith in Christ with others may not appear to be sprouting whatsoever. It may in fact lie there for months, years, or decades. In some cases, our lives on earth will end and we will be buried in the ground ourselves when suddenly that seed planted long ago bursts forth!

It puts down roots. It breaks through the hard ground. It begins to bud and flower and bring forth fruit. It is not late—but right on time according to the plan of our sovereign God. And remember, whenever a seed of the gospel takes root and grows, it is a miracle every single time.

We Are Truly Clueless

Stories like these force us to realize that not only are we not in control but we sometimes vastly underestimate what the Lord has in store in his divine plan. One of my favorite quotes from John Piper is this:

> *In every situation, God is always doing a thousand different things that you cannot see and you do not know.*[6]

It is stunning to think how little we know about any given situation. Perhaps you have heard the illustration about the multitudes of twisted threads on the back of a tapestry. It is only when the piece is turned to the front that we see the beautiful art that has been meticulously crafted. When we see twisted circumstances playing out now, we have no way to know how the Lord is crafting them by his divine plan into a masterpiece.

Could it be that this is one of the ways he purposefully shows us his attribute of *omniscience*, meaning that he know all things? We should give thanks daily for his all-knowing, all-seeing character.

In fact, why not stop right now and thank him for seeing all, knowing all, and sovereignly controlling all.

Precious Prodigals

Many parents of prodigals—beloved children who have turned away from the Lord—would likely admit that the massive weight of care they feel for their own lost children hinders their thankfulness to God for who he is. Whether they became Christians after their children were raised, or they prayed for salvation from the time their children were *in utero*, the pain of watching one's own child reject the gospel is difficult to adequately put into words.

So here's the plan: *we pray without ceasing.* We act like the one Jesus describes in Matthew 7, who is constantly asking, seeking, and knocking. Every time you think of those who are lost, pray for them by name instead of worrying about them. The God of the universe wants to hear from us and will not tire of us begging him repeatedly with the same plea for a lost sheep. And let's remember, he loves that lost sheep even more than we do.

Allow yourself to dream about what the Lord may be doing in their lives unseen to all at this very moment. Pray for people to be dropped right in their path. Read books about former prodigals whose testimonies are being used to reach those who are unlikely to listen to someone who has never known a stage of life away from the Lord. One book that I have found to be particularly helpful is James Banks' *Prayers for Prodigals*. It is a 90-day guide that can be repeated over and over again as we pray Scripture for our children.

But at the end of the day, this is a trust issue. Do we trust God, or not? Do we really believe that he created and loves every human being, and that he delights in saving souls through the shed blood of his Son? We can find it hard to press on when we see no progress. This is why our thankfulness to the Lord gets stalled, as we can become overwhelmed with a feeling of helplessness when we see the direction that those precious children seem to be heading. So much is at stake!

We must learn to remind ourselves that when we admit our utter helplessness, we are driven to also admit our utter dependence on our sovereign God, who loves us and our children. He is teaching us and them tough lessons that would not be learned under different circumstances.

How we all delight to hear accounts of prodigals who have come home and embraced Christ. We thrill to hear the circumstances that the Lord used to turn those wayward souls so that they are now sharing their faith with others, serving the local church, or perhaps answering God's call to missions. The puzzle pieces begin to fall into place as we get a glimpse of how God used the circumstances of those years of unbelief to prepare that person to fulfill a role that only he or she can fill. Praise God!

At Least She Got to Keep the Dog

My friend Rosaria Butterfield has had an interesting life, shall we say. Raised by a feminist, she grew up to become the head of the English department at a large, secular university. She had all the academic credentials for such a post and was well respected by faculty and students. She actively lobbied for LGBT causes alongside her lesbian partner.

Then an elderly pastor and his wife were given the opportunity to spend time with her. They hosted her in their home and, over the course of several years, lived out the gospel even as they challenged her to read the Bible. She began to visit their church, and eventually came by faith and repentance to a saving knowledge in the Lord Jesus Christ.

And this was God's plan all along!

Can you imagine the reaction at that university? Utter shock and disbelief. She says she "lost everything but the dog." My friend is now married to a pastor and homeschools her children in addition to being an author and speaker. The Lord shows us in remarkable ways how he is able to do above and beyond what we ask or think. I just love to read my friend's writings and hear her speak. She is an articulate, clear voice for biblical truth. She now puts her sharp intellect to use for the gospel in the public square. The Lord is using her in such a powerful way to the praise of his great name.

Yes, that was his plan all along. Yet many of us might have foolishly seen her as someone who would never listen to biblical truth. She seemed too radical, too politically extreme, too hostile toward the gospel. Shame on us! God called her away from her unbelief, and in the process transformed her just as he transforms all believers.

Let's be clear, we were all just as hopelessly lost as she was. However, she now has credibility to speak to those who are still living in the sin of homosexuality in a way that most of us cannot.

Work Is in Progress

We must take immense encouragement as we trust the Lord with our lost ones. Their stories are still unfolding in ways we cannot see. In our finite understanding, we have no way to see what God is preparing. So, we keep on sharing the good news, keep on praying, and keep on trusting the Lord for the results.

The apostle Paul is a stellar example of how God's plans are not our own:

> *I thank him who has given me strength, Christ Jesus our Lord, because he judged me faithful, appointing me to his service, though formerly I was a blasphemer,*

> *persecutor, and insolent opponent. But I received mercy*
> *because I had acted ignorantly in unbelief, and the*
> *grace of our Lord overflowed for me with the faith and*
> *love that are in Christ Jesus. The saying is trustworthy*
> *and deserving of full acceptance, that Christ Jesus*
> *came into the world to save sinners, of whom I am the*
> *foremost.*   1 TIMOTHY 1:12-15

Not only did Paul reject the gospel but he relentlessly persecuted the early church. But in Acts 9, we
read the amazing account of Christ himself appearing
to Paul. Everything changed. The Lord had planned
all along for Paul to be his "chosen instrument" to
take the gospel to the Jews (Acts 9:15). If you know
the story, you'll know that Paul became known as the
greatest Christian who ever lived. We read, study, and
memorize his writings which have been inspired by the
Holy Spirit and preserved for us in the Bible. How we
give glory to the Lord for saving Paul! The passage in
1 Timothy goes on to say this:

> *But I received mercy for this reason, that in me, as*
> *the foremost, Jesus Christ might display his **perfect***
> ***patience** as an example to those who were to believe*
> *in him for eternal life.*
>   1 TIMOTHY 1:16, *(bold text mine)*

Praise God for his perfect patience. How likely is it
that, if we had known Paul prior to his conversion,

we would have dared to predict how his life would radically change? I fear we would have been all too quick to consider him beyond the reach of salvation. What a horrible mistake that kind of thinking is for anyone then or now. *Jesus Christ is mighty to save and his power knows no bounds.*

Do you believe that?

Paul did. And so, even in the midst of his anguish for the Israelites (Romans 9), he could remind himself that God's ways are so much higher than ours, and can be trusted:

> *Oh, the depth of the riches and wisdom and knowledge of God! How unsearchable are his judgments and how inscrutable his ways!*
>
> *"For who has known the mind of the Lord, or who has been his counselor?"*
> *"Or who has given a gift to him that he might be repaid?"*
>
> *For from him and through him and to him are all things. To him be glory forever. Amen.*
>
> ROMANS 11:33-36

Like Paul, Christians are wonderfully able to know, even in the anguish of seeing people reject Christ, the gratitude of knowing that Christ is at work—and that his ways are higher than ours, always.

What If Loved Ones Have Died?

Words are inadequate to describe the grief of those whose loved one dies and appears to have not known Jesus Christ as Savior. Let's always be mindful that only God can judge the human heart. It is possible that our loved one confessed Jesus as Lord in the final moments of his or her life, unbeknown to us. How kind of the Holy Spirit to inspire Luke to include the words of Luke 23:43. This short verse tells us with certainty how the thief on the cross next to Jesus was redeemed. Jesus told him he would be with him in paradise. Praise God for the fact that he chooses to save some at the point of death, and that was his plan for them all along.

Our deepest comfort comes as we run to Scripture and are reminded of the unchanging nature of God. He is good and upright (Psalm 25:8). His steadfast love never ceases and his mercies never come to an end (Lamentations 3:22). He is both just and the justifier (Romans 3:26). "And we know that for those who love God all things work together for good, for those who are called according to his purpose" (Romans 8:28). We meditate deeply on these familiar yet profound truths.

Remember how Abraham pleaded with God in Genesis 18 to spare the righteous within the city of Sodom? As Abraham rightly asks, "Shall not the Judge of all the earth do what is just?" (Genesis 18:25). This much we know—our just and loving God rules over every person, situation, and circumstance now and forever for our good and his glory. And we rest in that. It is enough.

Unimpaired Thankfulness

As my new framed artwork says, we aim to start each day with a grateful heart, but let's not let it end there. As we think of loved ones who are, right now, living their lives with no regard for God, may we resolve to turn them over to the sovereign care of the Lord such that our thankfulness is not impaired.

We still have several other hindrances to explore and conquer in coming chapters but this one may be our hardest. Don't let it rob you of your joy in the Lord or squash your gratitude to him. *Trust the Lord.*

Stop and Pray

If your gratitude is hindered by fear for loved ones who do not know the Lord, would you stop and pray this prayer, or one of your own, now?

> *Gracious Father in heaven,*
>
> *I praise you for who you are. I cannot begin to comprehend your power, wisdom, and might, but I believe you are Almighty God.*
>
> *Thank you for sending your perfect Son, Jesus Christ, to die in my place so that I now stand forgiven forever.*
>
> *I want to grow in my walk with you, but I admit that my praise for you is hindered by the nagging fact that _____ rejects you and does not know you as Savior and Lord. I cannot imagine eternity away from your presence, and desperately beg you to draw _____ to yourself and save him/her.*

Help me to know what to say and what not to say in the meantime; and place in the path of this dear one other believers who will speak the truth of the gospel plainly.

It is so hard to wait! Give me patience as I wait for you to work out your perfect plan. Forgive my sin of wanting to be in control. Increase my faith as I trust in you alone to accomplish what you alone can do.

Help me to remember what you say in your word in Isaiah 55:8—"my thoughts are not your thoughts, neither are your ways my ways."

You are God alone. I praise you in the name of Jesus Christ, my Lord. Amen.

Think It Through

1. Is there someone who immediately comes to mind as you think about those who reject Christ? Do you allow your deep sorrow over this to rob your joy for what Christ has done for you? Confess that sin even as you continue to relentlessly pray for salvation for your loved one.

2. Have you thought about how God may be growing *you* in the process of waiting? Does your lack of control over the situation serve to drive you closer to the Lord or further away?

Too Busy To Bother?

The encounter happened years ago but I remember it so clearly. As I rounded the corner from one aisle to the next in a local grocery store, I almost literally ran into a friend whom I had not seen in years. We eagerly greeted each other, but I think "hello" was the only word that I could contribute to the conversation. She immediately launched into a monologue to inform me how busy and successful she was, and how she did not have a free moment even now to spare, although she spent at least two minutes telling me all about her current circumstances.

Just as quickly as we met that day, she was gone in a flurry. As she wheeled away with her cart, I remember thinking, "She has no idea if my entire family has just been wiped out." She did not have the time to listen but only to speak. And I think she left feeling sure that she had impressed me with just how busy she was— yet failed to realize how rude she was. But busyness equals success, right?

Wrong.

We live in an increasingly fast-paced society, so we must be careful not to evaluate our days based on how much we got done and how many boxes we checked off on our to-do lists. A huge hindrance to expressing gratitude to the Lord can be traced to our overbooked schedules and the self-focus that often follows.

What does it say to the Lord when we cannot carve out even a moment to thank him for the blessings he freely gives us? Or when we do so only as we are exhausted and falling asleep in our beds? It says that we have ungrateful hearts that are preoccupied with the distracting details of our lives.

This is nothing new.

Where Are the Other Nine?

In Luke 17 we read the account of Jesus healing ten lepers:

> *On the way to Jerusalem [Jesus] was passing along between Samaria and Galilee. And as he entered a village, he was met by ten lepers, who stood at a distance and lifted up their voices, saying, "Jesus, Master, have mercy on us." When he saw them he said to them, "Go and show yourselves to the priests."*

> *And as they went they were cleansed. Then one of*
> *them, when he saw that he was healed, turned back,*
> *praising God with a loud voice; and he fell on his*
> *face at Jesus' feet, giving him thanks. Now he was*
> *a Samaritan. Then Jesus answered, "Were not ten*
> *cleansed? Where are the nine? Was no one found to*
> *return and give praise to God except this foreigner?"*
> *And he said to him, "Rise and go your way; your*
> *faith has made you well."*   LUKE 17:11-19

These ten men had been afflicted with the horrid disease of leprosy. They were ostracized from their families as well as from society and lived a miserable existence. They begged Jesus to have mercy on them. He told them to go and show themselves to the priests and, *as they went*, they were cleansed.

Did you catch that phrase tucked inside this amazing story? *As they went*, healing took place immediately and the men were cleansed. Can you imagine these ten men rushing along and suddenly realizing that they were indeed clean? They pulled off the coverings and discovered the ugly skin sores were gone. The muscle pain in their legs had vanished. Their claw-like hands could now bend freely. They were no longer outcasts. Their nightmare was over. Jesus had healed them.

But only one turned around and went back to thank the one they had called "Master." We can hope that we would be the one who went back in this situation, right? Surely we would not be so preoccupied with getting to those priests to be declared clean that we would not turn around and thank the Lord?

But today, how often do we allow Satan to distract us with busyness and seemingly important tasks, such that our minds are always occupied with other things? We seem to have no time for anything more than a tip-of-the-hat type of gratitude as we quickly pray over our food. The Lord knows we are thankful, right? Our personal spiritual disciplines do not get the priority they deserve. We quickly read a passage of Scripture looking for some inspirational nugget to get us through the day, and then move on to the next task.

And we have been cured of something so much worse than the horrors of leprosy! We were dead in our sins and separated from God (Ephesians 2:1, 12).

Busyness Is Not the Goal

I find it easy to get defensive and show friends how busy I am doing good things. Maybe you do too. So I am on a campaign to stop the glorification of "busy" and to encourage taking a step back to re-evaluate how we spend our days. We need to be honest enough to admit when we are purely self-absorbed.

We are rightly concerned about taking care of our physical health, and that's wise, but are we concerned that stunted *spiritual* growth has consequences too? Busyness is often the fruit of good intentions. It does not reflect a deliberate rejection of God's great blessings to us—but the results are the same when we habitually rush or neglect our thanksgiving to the Lord, who gives us every hour.

This may come as a surprise if we've been too busy to give it much thought! When, as Christians, we neglect the things of the Lord by allowing them to get bumped from the day by more pressing tasks, we show ingratitude to the Lord. This hindrance is perhaps easier to fix than the others but it is no less urgent.

This too is a form of spiritual warfare, as we will see with each hindrance to gratitude that we identify. Satan is crafty and insightful. If he can convince us that we are busy doing good things, he can trick us into believing that time spent in prayer and Bible-study are less than essential. We start to rationalize that we have been good stewards of our time doing good things for the Lord. There is always tomorrow. We will try harder.

Progress Comes with a Price

The hectic pace of life in the twenty-first century would be difficult to explain to our great-grandmothers. The concepts of a smartphone loaded with time-saving tools and of social-media apps would be lost on them. Yes, we enjoy some amazing conveniences today. But, without restraint, social media alone can eat up hours of time every day (as well as feeding envy when we believe the often sugar-coated scenarios that are posted).

Our ancestors would be amazed at the schedules we keep with kids in multiple activities simultaneously such that the family rarely has a meal together. The thought of starting Christmas shopping in September before it reaches a fever pitch in December would not even make sense to them. Sadly, with much of that progress have come untold stress and the desire to cram our lives full until we are exhausted. We could learn a great deal from our grandmothers by dialing it back a bit and perhaps doing fewer things well instead of doing more things with mediocrity. We must not let this slide. In his very helpful book, *Crazy Busy*, Kevin DeYoung closes with these words:

> *It's not wrong to be tired. It's not wrong to feel*
> *overwhelmed. It's not wrong to go through seasons*
> *of complete chaos. What is wrong—and is*
> *heartbreakingly foolish and wonderfully avoidable—is*
> *to live a life with more craziness than we want because*
> *we have less Jesus than we need.*[7]

Let that never be said of us. Defy Satan. Don't let him persuade you to neglect gratitude for the sake of your schedule.

Avoiding the Epidemic of Self-Absorption

Sometimes we are so self-absorbed with the pressure cooker in which we find ourselves that we have little concern for others, let alone a consistent awareness of the Lord's presence and provision. It is almost as though we want others to be amazed at all of the plates we have spinning in the air. What an unbiblical attitude!

Do nothing from selfish ambition or conceit, but in
humility count others more significant than yourselves.

PHILIPPIANS 2:3

Do you know anyone who lives in a small, constricted world? (It may be that this someone is *you*, at times.) They may not even be very busy by most people's definition. Yet the circumstances they encounter on any given day are all-encompassing. They struggle to look outside of their daily lives to see those around them who are truly in need. This self-absorbed mentality is such a hindrance to gratitude.

May we be intentional about modeling for others that we seek to be outward-focused. By God's grace, we want to be, first and foremost, grateful to the Lord for who is he and what he has done. And we sincerely desire to encourage others as we "rejoice with those who rejoice [and] weep with those who weep" (Romans 12:15). It is impossible to do so if we cannot see past our own circumstances.

Reality Check from Africa

My husband serves as the president of a large theological seminary. We have had the privilege for 25 years of embracing and equipping students and their families as they prepare for ministry in the US and around the world. One such family recently launched into the mission field in Africa along with their seven young children. One of their early prayer requests was for consistent electricity and running water.

As I considered what it must be like with to have seven children and only sporadic power and water, not only was I convicted of the need to pray for them but I marveled with shame at how rarely I give thanks to the Lord that when I turn on the faucet, clean water comes gushing out. When I flip on a switch, there is power. On the rare occasions when water or power fail, how terribly inconvenienced I feel as I scramble to find out when they will be restored.

I was further taken out of my self-focus when I emailed my friend to tell her that I was praying for her and got this reply:

> *It is amazing how surroundings change perspective. Even after simplifying life significantly, we are still living like kings in comparison, and still counted among the richest in the world. I am less comfortable than I've ever been, but more content and grateful. I am realizing entitlement has been the root of my struggle with giving thanks in all circumstances. I have embraced the truth that just because I am an American doesn't mean I am entitled to live better than anyone else. I just don't want you or anyone to admire us as if we are to be pitied or for anyone to feel shamed for enjoying running water ... as long as they know they aren't entitled to running water either.*

What a wise woman! How I thank God for her sweet attitude that slays entitlement and embraces contentment. She is not looking for admiration nor pity but she is absolutely right with her reminder that we are not *entitled* to anything either.

This takes us back once again to gracious gratitude. We are completely dependent on our all-powerful God, who generously gives us every gift we possess. He owes us nothing but condemnation. We owe him everything—including hearts that brim with great thankfulness.

Thought Control

Sometimes busyness gives way to the sheer weariness of a homemaker's routine as she is tempted to feel defeated by the monotony of the same tasks over and over again while caring for a young family. This thought process can start a downward spiral that is neither healthy nor productive. However, Paul encourages us to refocus our minds on everything that is good—and this will lead, in turn, to knowing God's peace:

> *Finally, brothers, whatever is true, whatever is honorable, whatever is just, whatever is pure, whatever is lovely, whatever is commendable, if there is any excellence, if there is anything worthy of praise, think about these things. What you have learned and received and heard and seen in me— practice these things, and the God of peace will be with you.* PHILIPPIANS 4:8-9

So let's be intentional about stalling unhealthy thoughts and looking for ways to turn them into grateful thoughts.

Here is a simple example that I now find myself thinking when I turn on the dishwasher. I referred to grandmothers earlier in this chapter. Both of my grandmothers were farmers' wives with large families. How grateful they would have been for a microwave, a stand-mixer, or an ice-maker. And what about a dishwasher? I did not even have a large family, but I am very thankful for electric dishwashers even now as an empty-nester. After loading the dishes, I place that little soap tablet in the door and push start. Maybe I am weird, but I like to hear the tablet drop out of the compartment as it begins to do its job. When I hear it drop, I thank the Lord that I do not have to wash and dry any of those dishes. He has allowed me to live in an era when I can push a button and the work will be done. I also seek to be mindful that although many homes have dishwashers in my country, such conveniences are unheard of in many parts of the world.

No Big Grins Required

We do enjoy many gifts that our ancestors did not. What's your favorite convenience? Maybe it is your washer and your dryer. As you run them for the fourth time today, are you grateful that you do not have to scrub garments on a washing board or hang wet clothes on a clothesline? Or do you grumble because, as the laundry is done and put away, there will already be newly-soiled clothes in the hamper?

I am not suggesting that we run around with big, dumb grins on our faces, thanking God for laundry soap that works in cool machines. I am suggesting that it is a wise exercise to look for ways to be grateful in the seemingly small things, especially when we find ourselves being discontent about our particular routines and circumstances. Being thankful for the small things is a great entry into turning our thoughts around and focusing them on the Lord. If we have a mindset of gratitude even while carrying out the routine tasks of our day, we will find we have fewer thoughts of complaint and self-focus. This has been true for me. Ever since I took to heart the prayer request from my friend with seven children for just a few hours of water, I try to think differently when I turn on the faucet at home.

Striking a Balance

It is not wrong to be busy. If we swing too far in the other direction, we become idle. We all know some people whom we'd like to encourage to roll up their sleeves and become more active in gospel work. We know the Bible frowns upon idleness in several places, including in the description of the Proverbs 31 woman who is commended because she "does not eat the bread of idleness" (Proverbs 31:27).

Jesus was certainly busy and not idle. He lived the perfect life and thus struck a perfect balance between the two. How many times are we told that he went off to a quiet place to pray (for example, Matthew 14:23, Mark 1:35)? He made time in prayer with his Father a priority no matter how busy or tired he was. It's all a matter of our attitude. Consider this quote from *A Praying Life* by Paul Miller:

> *The quest for a contemplative life can actually be self-absorbed, focused on quiet and me. If we love people and have the power to help, then we are going to be busy. Learning to pray does not offer us a less busy life; it offers us a less busy heart. In the midst of outer busyness we can develop an inner quiet. Because we are less hectic on the inside, we have a greater capacity to love ... and thus to be busy, which in turn drives us even more into a life of prayer.*[8]

I so want to discipline myself to have a less busy *heart* filled with an inner quiet: one that reflects the delicate balance between idleness and frenzy.

Wrapping It Up

We are grateful that the Lord gives us good work to do every day coupled with the energy to carry it out. That's so healthy! But may we resolve not to let our gratitude start and end there, such that busyness is the hallmark of our days.

We desire to be the caring friend at the store who would not be so busy that we brush someone off. We desire to be like the healed leper who ran back to thank Jesus. We desire to be the woman who works to consistently be mindful of blessings big and small—like dishwasher tablets. We desire to defy Satan when he seeks to throw us off course. We desire to do as Scripture plainly teaches:

> *Look carefully then how you walk, not as unwise but as wise, making the best use of the time, because the days are evil.* Ephesians 5:15-16

Let this be our prayer!

Dear Father in heaven,

I confess my sins of selfishness and self-absorption. I further confess that I sometimes fall into the busyness trap in hopes of pleasing people by trying to do it all.

As a result, I fall miserably short of pleasing you, my Creator, by failing to make a priority of expressing gratitude for who you are and what you have done for me.

Please help me to eagerly look at each day as an opportunity to know you better and obey you more faithfully. I want to redeem the time!

Thank you for each and every busy day that I get to spend on earth. May I be available and never too busy for whatever kingdom tasks you send my way.

In the name of my precious Savior, Jesus Christ, do I pray. Amen.

Think It Through

1. Could you possibly be described as someone like the lady I saw at the grocery store? Are you sometimes so self-absorbed that you ignore others in careless ways—and even neglect time with the Lord? Resolve to make course corrections today.

2. Does Satan succeed in persuading you to think unhealthy thoughts instead of grateful ones? Thought therapy is vital! Look for ways to be thankful for simple things at every turn, and ask the Lord to bring them joyfully to mind daily.

If Only Life Were Different...

So far, we have considered two hindrances to gratitude—the rejection of the gospel by those we love, and the way Satan distracts us with busyness and self-focus. Another hindrance comes when we allow discontent over circumstances to rob us of both joy and thankfulness. Sometimes we are tempted to believe we would be more grateful if we did not have to walk in our own heavy shoes. We allow suffering to define us, and, when we do this, Satan wins.

You may have heard the amazing testimony of Joni Eareckson Tada. She is a remarkable woman who has lived for more than 50 years as a quadriplegic and has triumphed through six rounds of chemotherapy with stage-3 breast cancer. I had the privilege of meeting her recently when she and her husband, Ken, visited our campus and spoke to our students.

Joni knows all about suffering but it is not her life story. She is a victorious Christian woman who claims the promise that God's power is perfected in weakness (2 Corinthians 12:9). He has gifted her to spread the gospel message from her wheelchair. I was struck by her words after a particularly bad day of chemo. She first said that her suffering that day was like a "splash-over of hell"—one that inspired gratitude because she knows she will not live like this forever. But upon further reflection, she concluded that her suffering was much more like a "splash-over of heaven"—defined as "finding Jesus in the splash-over of hell."[9] I will never forget that word picture.

What Credibility Do I Bring?

Joni is a gifted author who has written many fine books on the subject of **suffering**. The Lord has uniquely equipped her to do so as she lives victoriously in spite of the pain. And she has graciously used her suffering to serve her brothers and sisters in Christ around the world.

In contrast, who am I to write even a single chapter about discontent and suffering? I am blessed with remarkably good health. I sleep like a baby. I have never been injured in an accident. I rarely get a headache. I have never gone to bed scared or hungry.

I am mindful this is not the norm, and I regularly thank the Lord for his unmerited favor to me, including protection from trauma as well as my physical and mental heath. But I also realize that every day is a gift. Not one of us knows what kind of cells are growing in our bodies even now, nor what wayward vehicle may lurk around the bend tomorrow. By the time this book is published, my life could be radically different. That's not pessimistic but it is realistic. It is possible that I will continue to enjoy health and safety, but if not, I must be ready to respond in a God-honoring way that seeks to be content in all circumstances (Philippians 4:12). And so I desire to think through this topic carefully even as I am mindful of those who are walking through great adversity now.

Mom with a Message

Many of us care for family members who suffer. The profound sense of grief and pain seems overwhelming as we watch and pray. I heard the story of a well-meaning chaplain who visited a young boy near death from brain cancer. The chaplain said to the child's mother, "Listen, as we go through this, I want you to know that God is not involved in this. Now, he will help you on the other side but this is one of those things that God is not involved in."

The mother looked him squarely in the eyes and said, "You may be trying to comfort me but I get no comfort from that. I've got to believe that God's hand is here and I'm going to trust that. I don't know how I'm going to bear up emotionally but he is not absent; he has not blinked; and this is not happening apart from him. My God is at work—for he takes and he gives, he gives and he takes. I am asking him for faith to bless his name."

That chaplain was given an education that day from a mother whose heart was breaking but who was successfully able to trust God's heart even when she could not see his hand. Praise God that he revealed his wisdom to her so that through her grief, her words now resound in our ears.

These wonderful truths come from Romans 8:28; Psalm 23:4; Psalm 37:28; Job 1:21; and 1 Peter 5:10. They speak to the nature of our unfailing God, who is indeed involved and at work even in the deepest valley. And these truths help us do what the Lord enabled that mother to do—to trust his *heart* even when we cannot see his *hand*.

Those Pesky Thorns Must Be Handled

We can only walk in our own shoes, so we don't know the half of what some bear from physical, emotional, or economic burdens. You may hear such burdens called one's "thorn in the flesh," a phrase used by the apostle Paul when writing about his own situation.

Those painful thorns are constantly present for many who struggle every day to push through. As Paul writes:

> *So to keep me from becoming conceited ... **a thorn was given me in the flesh**, a messenger of Satan to harass me, to keep me from becoming conceited.*

*Three times I pleaded with the Lord about this, that
it should leave me. But he said to me, "My grace
is sufficient for you, for my power is made perfect
in weakness." Therefore I will boast all the more
gladly of my weaknesses, so that the power of Christ
may rest upon me. For the sake of Christ, then,
I am content with weaknesses, insults, hardships,
persecutions, and calamities. For when I am weak,
then I am strong.*

2 Corinthians 12:7-10 *(bold text mine)*

I heard Dr. Heath Lambert make an excellent point
as he preached on this text in our seminary's chapel.[10]
To paraphrase him, he said Paul was arguably the greatest Christian who ever lived. The Holy Spirit inspired
Paul to write so much of the New Testament such that
we rightly devour his words centuries later. Paul had a
short life on earth to accomplish so much. Wouldn't
he, of all people, have been able to thrive had he not
been afflicted with this thorn, whatever it was? *Well,
apparently not.* Three times he asked the Lord to take
it away and three times the Lord did not. Since he did
not take it away, it must be that our infinitely wise and
powerful God determined that the apostle Paul should
not be relieved of his great difficulty.

Great point! We should therefore not question the
presence of our own thorns but continue to pray for
relief as we trust God in all things. Since he did not
remove Paul's thorn, it may be his plan not to remove

ours either. I know this is much easier said than done, but we will understand it all in glory.

When we question our plight, it is much like looking at a map and saying, "Lord, if only I could go down this road, it would be so much faster and more convenient." But the Lord directs us down a different road—one that looks long and treacherous. When we get to heaven, will it not be amazing to see how that seemingly easy road would have been a disaster? Whereas we will find that the people we met and the things we did and the lessons we learned along the road we walked were unmistakably the best path for us.

Praying Scripture

Do you suffer from affliction that hampers your gratitude? One of the best remedies is to pray Scripture. It is so powerful to pray to the Lord the words he has carefully preserved for us in his precious word. *Praying the Bible* by Donald S. Whitney is a helpful book that lays out a simple plan that can be transformational. For example, try praying Psalm 51 to the Lord. It says in verse 12, "Restore to me the joy of your salvation, and uphold me with a willing spirit." Don't just read it. Pray it to the Lord with all sincerity! Don't stop until you truly mean what you are saying.

Paul and Peter both recorded amazing prayers that were inspired by the Holy Spirit and have been preserved for us by him. Look them up and make them your own! Philippians 1:3-11; Colossians 1:9-14;

1 Thessalonians 3:11-13; 2 Thessalonians 1:11-12; Ephesians 1:16-23; or 3:14-21: these references will take you to some of them. These prayers to our same Father can become a lifeline as we pray them with all earnestness in Jesus' name.

Outcome-Based Suffering

After Paul's prayer in the first chapter of Philippians, he says this:

> *I want you to know, brothers, that what has happened to me has really served to advance the gospel, so that it has become known throughout the whole imperial guard and to all the rest that my imprisonment is for Christ. And most of the brothers, having become confident in the Lord by my imprisonment, are much more bold to speak the word without fear.*

PHILIPPIANS 1:12-14

Let's not miss this striking comment about the results of Paul's suffering. What an amazing perspective Paul has trained himself to embrace as he concludes that the gospel has been advanced through hardship. He noted "outcome-based results" centuries before such a thing was in vogue. He could have chosen to retell the many harrowing experiences of his suffering as he wrote this letter from jail, but instead he jumps to the happy conclusion that the gospel is moving forward. The whole imperial guard is aware of Paul's mission. His boldness in the midst of suffering is serving to make his brothers bolder too. Win-win.

Seeking to be mindful of who God is and how much he loves us will help us rightly interpret our personal circumstances. The alternative is flawed thinking that starts with our circumstances and attempts to interpret God's love and care, or seeming lack thereof, from there. Even when the details do not make sense to us, we can train ourselves, with the Lord's help, to trust in his unfailing love for us. We must never let our suffering define us, but rather, resolve to allow God to use it to make us victorious as it too—as with Paul's—will advance the gospel in ways we would never imagine.

A lovely example of this comes from a most unlovely place—the World War II concentration camp at Ravensbrück, in northern Germany. Corrie ten Boom and her sister Betsie had been caught saving Jewish families from the Nazi genocide. They were imprisoned at Ravensbrück, crammed into disgusting, foul-smelling barracks built for 400 but housing 1400 instead. In this terrible place, Betsie encouraged her sister to find as much as possible to give thanks for. But when Betsie thanked God even for the fleas, it was too much for Corrie. Not fleas! How could she thank God for being bitten?

The sisters had smuggled a small Bible into the camp, so each evening they read it aloud to growing groups of women. It was against the rules, but day after day no guards came round the barracks. Everywhere else they were watched all the time, but not in Barracks 28. This extra freedom allowed Corrie and Betsie to run two Bible groups instead of one, so that many more women could hear the precious word of God.

After several weeks, Betsie discovered the reason for their freedom. No guard or supervisor would enter their barracks—for fear of being bitten. The sisters hadn't known it at the time, but Betsie had been right to thank God for fleas!

Could We Smile through the Pain?

I will never forget Bobbie. Her battle with cancer was reaching an end and she was preparing to meet Jesus face to face. Yet her face was radiant, and her smile was captivating, even as she occasionally winced in pain as she changed positions in her chair.

Our discussion moved to the obvious topic of her suffering. I commended her attitude in enduring so many surgeries, procedures, and treatments in hope of being cured. There was no shred of bitterness in her voice as she spoke of her prognosis. Her faith was unwavering. Her gratitude to God was undiminished. She was spending her last days making as many memories with her precious family and a host of friends as was possible. I was in awe as she mentioned her non-Christian oncologist with whom she relentlessly spoke of Christ even as she lived out the gospel before that doctor's eyes.

Bobbie showed no fear of death whatsoever due to her calm assurance of a life hidden with Christ in

God forever (Colossians 3:3). Bobbie would not let me dwell on her situation though. She wanted to know about me and my struggles. She wanted to know what specific needs she could take before the Lord on my behalf as she prayed in her red quiet-time chair during the days she had remaining.

We prayed together that day through tears. As we parted, I remember thinking I would want to be just like her if this happened to me. In the midst of a devastating trial I would want to have peace that not only buoyed me but encouraged others and drew them to Christ. Bobbie taught me it was possible to do so.

Careful Thinkers

So here's the bottom line as we think about how suffering can be an obstacle to gracious gratitude. Does our lot in life affect our ability to show gratitude to God? Are we unable to truly celebrate the attributes of God if we are injured or physically ill or depressed or unemployed or single or childless or unloved—to name a few trials we may face?

If we are honest, we will admit that it seems easier to praise God for his nature when we feel as if things are going reasonably well. We can try to rationalize that our lot is better than most and so we should pull ourselves together and be grateful. But beware of flawed thinking! We must battle our sinful natures every day as we retrain our thought processes. Good habits take time to form just as bad ones do. We must think first of God's perfect love for us—and then reflect on the circumstances. If we get it backwards, we consider the circumstances first—and start to question God's perfect love for us.

Our time on this earth is but a blip. Even when your suffering seems overwhelming, please do not let it define who you are. Meditate on clear passages like Romans 5. It may seem impossible that you can "rejoice in your sufferings" but only the Lord can enable you to do so. He will use it to produce endurance, character, and hope (Romans 5:3)!

Are you grateful today for the unchangeable and absolute truth that our God is holy and righteous? He is worthy to be praised in all circumstances—not *for* all circumstances but *in* them. Paul is very plain in the closing words of his first letter to the church at Thessalonica:

> [16] *Rejoice always,* [17] *pray without ceasing,* [18] *give thanks in all circumstances; for this is the will of God in Christ Jesus for you.* 1 THESSALONIANS 5:16-18

We need not be Greek scholars to understand this. It is clear and to the point: *rejoice, pray, give thanks.* Further, rejoice all the time, don't stop praying, and give thanks in all circumstances. Since this command is in God's word, that means it is for all of us. However, the phrase at the end of verse 18 provides great insight. *Why* are we supposed to do these things? We do them because this is God's will for us in Christ Jesus.

This is simple, but it is not oversimplified. Whole books are written on how to know the will of God for your life. Paul cuts to the chase. Pray, rejoice, give thanks. We give thanks as we serve the God who loves us more than we can ever imagine. It is his will for each one of us to do so no matter what our circumstances.

Pray. Rejoice. Give thanks.

Father,

Give us the courage to resist the prowling lion that seeks to devour, as Peter described Satan in 1 Peter 5.

You have bought us with a price—the life of your one and only Son. You love us and are working through us to accomplish your will.

Make us mindful that our suffering is indeed for a little while, even when it seems fierce and unending.

You are God. We are not. We praise you with our whole hearts and magnify your name. Please give us even a glimpse of your providence through our suffering. May that glimpse remind us that you are at work.

In the name of Jesus, who suffered and died for us, we pray.

Amen.

Think It Through

1. Do you let your thorn in the flesh define who you are and diminish your capacity for gratitude as a result? No one can walk in your shoes, but can you perhaps find a believer who will stand alongside to encourage you and to pray for you in this specific area?

2. As you seek to allow the Lord to advance the gospel through your circumstances, have you tried praying through the book of Psalms on a regular basis? It can be transformational!

The Doubt-Slayer

Doubt and guilt are no strangers to most believers at some point in our journey. But these feelings can be another hindrance to gratitude, so in this chapter we will look at biblical passages to encourage us and biblical characters to inspire us. And along the way, we will ask how these make a difference to our lives.

Paid in Full

Imagine the scene in the courtroom as a guilty criminal's conviction is overturned. An innocent man has willingly, lovingly, and unconditionally accepted the penalty for the criminal's crime. The guilty man is declared innocent and allowed to go free. How can this be? He did not earn or deserve this free gift, nor can he begin to understand it. Surely this pardoned criminal would spend the rest of his life filled with the most profound gratitude possible. Would he not wear himself out telling everyone about the one who took his place?

So we would be shocked to hear that instead of gratitude for his freedom, he dwells on the past—his life before the crime, the crime itself, his time in prison—and on his guilt for not serving his sentence. He even wakes up at night fearful that the man who took his place will change his mind and his sentence will be reinstated. He should be the most joyful man on the planet. What's his problem?

We could ask ourselves the same question. As believers in the Lord Jesus Christ, we have been pardoned and the penalty for our sins has been paid in full. We have assurance of our salvation (John 10:28) and there is therefore now no condemnation for those who are in Christ Jesus (Romans 8:1). It seems that gratitude should overflow from our hearts such that our life before we knew Christ would not be a hindrance to thanksgiving.

Yet some believers allow guilt over their past to hover like a dark cloud.

Every Christian Has an Amazing Story to Tell

My story is one of those testimonies that some dare to call boring. Raised in a Christian home, I became a believer as a young child and the Lord has held me fast ever since. I have had no crisis of faith and was never tempted to go off the tracks. That is not to say that I am not a great sinner who serves a great Savior, to paraphrase the hymn-writer John Newton. And every day I realize my salvation is nothing short of miraculous. Only the Lord can work in our hearts and minds to turn us from his enemies into his daughters and sons (Colossians 1:21-22).

What's your story? Is it like mine? The complete opposite? Or somewhere in between?

I have some friends who had rough lives full of shameful acts of sin before Jesus called them to himself and saved them forever. Their experiences were a long way from my childhood conversion. Yet every one of us—whatever our story—is a new creation (2 Corinthians 5:17).

But Satan tries to convince us that we should still carry some guilt. The scars from sin resulting from one's life before Christ can get pushed to the forefront of the mind—sexual immorality, abortion, or maybe an outright rejection of God.

It's not wrong to experience doubt—many of us do— but it is a mistake if we fail to challenge our doubts by speaking the gospel truth to those doubts. As believers, we stand forgiven by God the Father through faith in Jesus Christ. God the Father looks at each one of us through Christ's death on the cross such that when he sees us, it is just as if we never sinned. And this doesn't just apply to those sins we committed before coming to faith but also to any we commit as Christians. This is wonderfully true for every one of us who is a believer. What a marvelous truth to hold onto when we doubt. How kind and loving our Father God is!

Sometimes, doubts come because we worry we cannot consistently live the holy lives we are called to. We see our failings and fear they will dim God's love for us. This is the time to grasp hold of gospel truth with both hands. We remind ourselves that we are right before God purely because of Christ. It is Christ's life which the Lord sees when he looks at us. Our forgiveness is certain. Our relationship with God is safe. So that's what we remind ourselves of, again and again if needed, when doubt tries to slay us.

Let's Talk Doctrine

This is not a book about doctrine—our core beliefs taken from Scripture. But some basic doctrines will help us as we consider the problems of guilt and doubt. We are *not* all called to be theologians but we *are* all called to be lifelong students of the Bible. This means we must use all of the tools we have to prayerfully seek to understand what God's word means and why that matters.

Jude clearly made the point that believers must hold fast to the faith:

> *I found it necessary to write appealing to you to* **contend for the faith** *that was once for all delivered to the saints.* JUDE 3, *(bold text mine)*

It is certainly more challenging to *contend for the faith* if we do not have a good grasp of what we believe and why we believe it. We will also be ripe for the picking by false teachers if we do not know what we believe and why. Paul makes this plain:

For the time is coming when people will not endure sound teaching, but having itching ears they will accumulate for themselves teachers to suit their own passions, and will turn away from listening to the truth and wander off into myths.   2 TIMOTHY 4:3-4

So, let's think briefly about the doctrine of justification. The Bible teaches that we are *justified* when we are declared righteous in the sight of God, pardoned from our sin, and promised eternal life solely through the work of Christ on the cross in taking the full penalty for our sin (Romans 5:1-11). The result is gloriously described in the New Hampshire Confession of Faith, penned in 1833:

... it (justification) brings us into a state of most blessed peace and favor with God, and secures every other blessing needful for time and eternity.

Here is one more helpful quote about justification:

Because our identity is founded in the resurrected Christ seated at God's right hand, God looks upon

us as being clothed with the perfection of his Son.
On this basis, we have the audacity to lift our eyes to
heaven in the absence of guilt and know that we are
accepted as sons and daughters of almighty God.[11]

It really is audacious for us to lift our eyes to heaven—but that's exactly what we are privileged to do because of Christ. How wonderful!

Providentially Speaking

Another doctrine to consider here is the providence of God.

And we know that for those who love God all things
work together for good, for those who are called
according to his purpose. ROMANS 8:28

God directs all things according to his perfect will. We cannot understand it now but we will someday. We are wise to refrain from trying to second-guess his plan, and instead rejoice in the fact that we serve a God who loves us and is in full control of all things. This providence covers our life stories.

What if all Christians had testimonies of being saved at an early age, and never drifted or doubted? And what if there were no believers who were called to Christ after decades of rebellion towards him and his word? In that case, there would be no real-life stories to encourage those who come to the Lord after doubt or drifting. But instead, the Lord in his providence uses the compelling life stories of those who walked in darkness for years to draw others to himself. He certainly hates the sin-filled lives of rejection embraced by unbelievers, but his glory is revealed in the amazing transformations of many that he ordained to be saved before time began.

Have you considered how *your* life story has been uniquely orchestrated by the Lord? He makes no mistakes.

We must all be intentional about showing gratitude to the Lord for his providence to us in creating us and then saving us in exactly the way he did. Be thankful that he knit you together in your mother's womb (Psalm 139:13) and that you are his:

> *But now thus says the LORD, he who created you, O Jacob, he who formed you, O Israel: "Fear not, for I have redeemed you; I have called you by name, you are mine."* ISAIAH 43:1

What grateful hearts we should have! He has redeemed us and calls us by name. We are his!

A Man after God's Own Heart

I struggled in the past to understand the story of David, and in particular how the Lord treated him after he committed adultery and murder. We read in the Old Testament about Uzzah, who touched the ark of the covenant and died (2 Samuel 6:1-7). We read in the New Testament about Ananias and Sapphira, who were struck dead on the spot for lying (Acts 5:1-11). These are just two examples of swift and sudden judgment for sin. *So why did this not happen to David?*

There is no disputing that David committed both adultery and murder (2 Samuel 11). However, in spite of David's great moral sin, Scripture describes him as a *man after God's own heart* (1 Samuel 13:14; Acts 13:22). Jesus is referred to as the "Son of David" no less than 17 times in the New Testament. He thus fulfilled the Old Testament prophecy that the Messiah would be born from the lineage of David. How can this be so, I wondered, given David's history?

God's word is not written to confuse or confound us. Digging deeper into these accounts brings clarity. Uzzah appears to have been trying to "assist" God. That was a really bad idea. Ananias and Sapphira were used as an example to show how much God hates flagrant sin. As a result, the early church learned a valuable lesson. This is not to minimize David's sin. We must carefully consider what the Lord seeks to teach us through each and every account of Scripture, and ask for his particular help to understand those that we find puzzling.

David's sin caused him to suffer greatly (2 Samuel 12:9-14). As a result of his sin, his own sons caused him great grief (2 Samuel 13 – 18). We are blessed to see how deep and profound David's repentance was, as recorded in Psalm 51.

For I know my transgressions,
and my sin is ever before me.
Against you, you only, have I sinned
and done what is evil in your sight ...

Hide your face from my sins,
and blot out all my iniquities.
Create in me a clean heart, O God,
and renew a right spirit within me.
Cast me not away from your presence,
and take not your Holy Spirit from me.
Restore to me the joy of your salvation,
and uphold me with a willing spirit.

PSALM 51:3-4, 9-12

The Lord allowed David to live long enough to see God's hand at work even in his sin and suffering. Scripture records many details about David's life as well more than 75 psalms written by David. We know that he had tremendous faith as the young boy who single-handedly killed Goliath. We know that he loved God's law and sought to follow it with his whole heart.

And let's be sure to note how much we learn about gratitude from David's inspired words in the psalms. Many have been quoted already in this book! Think about the millions upon millions of people who have been blessed as a result of the psalms of David, including Jesus himself, who quoted them. As David rejoiced in the forgiveness he received, he wrote these words:

> *You have turned for me my mourning into dancing;*
> *you have loosed my sackcloth*
> *and clothed me with gladness,*
> *that my glory may sing your praise and not be silent.*
> *O LORD my God, I will give thanks to you*
> *forever!*   PSALM 30:11-12

Is it not our desire for history to record that we have lived our lives in such a way that we are women after God's own heart? How encouraging to know that David earned his title even though he was a great sinner—a sinner who repented and found true forgiveness.

Paul: Chief among Sinners

Just as we give thanks for the words of David, we are no less thankful for the inspired words of Paul that we read, study, and memorize in his thirteen letters in the New Testament. He calls himself the chief, or foremost, among sinners (1 Timothy 1:15); yet the Lord appeared to him on the road to Damascus and saved him. At that point, Paul's days of persecuting Christians were over and he became arguably the greatest Christian who has ever lived.

Does that encourage you? Our Lord forgave a sinner like Paul and used him in ways that no one ever would have predicted. How can we do anything other than rejoice with great gratitude that he saved us from our sin as well, no matter what it was?

Satan Loves It When We Doubt

We see doubters crop up several times in the New Testament. When John the Baptist's father, Zechariah, was told by an angel that he would have a son, he doubted. So the angel told Zechariah that he would be mute until the baby was born. Zechariah thus had long months to ponder his decision to doubt God's word (Luke 1:18-23).

Perhaps the most famous doubter is still known centuries later—and by people who are not even students of the Bible—as "doubting Thomas." This disciple would not believe Jesus was resurrected unless he saw the nail marks with his own eyes and touched them with his own hands. Jesus then told Thomas, "Blessed are those who have not seen and yet have believed" (John 20:29). This includes us—and we are most certainly blessed!

We must have faith to believe what we cannot yet see or understand with our own finite knowledge. This faith is given to us as a gift from the Holy Spirit. Embrace it! Remember, without faith it is impossible to please God (Hebrews 11:6). Here's a great definition of faith found in Hebrews 11:

> *Now faith is the assurance of things hoped for, the conviction of things not seen.* HEBREWS 11:1

Satan loves to plant seeds of doubt in our minds. It is one of his most powerful weapons. He successfully persuaded Eve to doubt God's own words in Genesis 3. He tries to bombard us with thoughts of how we are unworthy to receive unmerited favor from the holy God. We must quickly dismiss such thoughts, asking God to help us if we find this hard, as we offer gratitude to God for saving us and putting our past behind us forever.

Meditate on these reassuring passages:

> *Remember not the former things, nor consider the things of old.* ISAIAH 43:18

> *But one thing I do: forgetting what lies behind and straining forward to what lies ahead, I press on toward the goal for the prize of the upward call of God in Christ Jesus.* PHILIPPIANS 3:13-14

The Big Picture

One great lesson we learn from the Bible over and over again is how God's purpose is being worked out in the midst of seemingly hopeless circumstances. God is perfectly conforming every situation to his perfect will. And he is good all the time. We can trust him. His plan is better than anything we could imagine.

Our response to the overwhelming grace we have received should be nothing less than overwhelming gratitude. We are wise to put away all of the "would have, could have, should have" thoughts about how we might have avoided past situations. God was in every single detail that happened prior to our salvation. Guilt has got to go. Our doubt about our future is just as foolish as the prisoner's worry that the one who took his place is going to change his mind. Let's go back to the epistle of Jude again. His doxology is priceless!

> *Now to him who is able to keep you from stumbling and to present you blameless before the presence of his glory with great joy, to the only God, our Savior, through Jesus Christ our Lord, be glory, majesty, dominion, and authority, before all time and now and forever. Amen.*　　　　　　　　JUDE 24-25

He who began a good work in us will be faithful to complete it (Philippians 1:6). Period.

> *Father, we praise you because you are able to keep us from stumbling!*
>
> *We look forward to that great day when Jesus will present us blameless before you.*
>
> *We cling to your promises and beg you to drive away all guilt from our life prior to salvation in Christ alone.*
>
> *Remove any doubt and make us mindful that it is the work of Satan.*
>
> *We will glorify your name and celebrate the fact that we are yours, bought with a price, and secure for all eternity.*
>
> *All because of Jesus, Amen.*

Think It Through

1. Do you allow past circumstances to play back in your mind over and over again like reruns? Have you prayed with all your might for the Lord to give you the ability to stop doing so and to help you instead to focus on the present and on his complete and perfect forgiveness?

2. Do you aspire to be a woman after God's own heart? What a tremendous title! Like David, we are forgiven from whatever we did in the past. There is no place for doubt! Pray for a heart filled with joy and gratitude that lives to please the Lord.

Thanking God When It Hurts

I love spring flowers. They are some of the most beautiful parts of God's creation. If money was no object, I would place vases filled with multi-colored bouquets all over the house. Roses are among the most beautiful and fragrant. We have no problem thanking the Lord for the beauty of every rose he allows us to enjoy, each one delicately created by our Creator in vibrant color.

Yet I cannot recall even one time when I thanked the Lord for placing sharp thorns along the stems of those beautiful flowers, and I'm guessing you can't either. There is nothing beautiful about those thorns, yet they are not there by accident. God chose to place them there—probably to protect the blooms from animals who may want to eat them.

Can We Be Thankful for Thorns?

So far, we have defined two levels of gratitude— *natural gratitude* (thanking God for his gifts) and *gracious gratitude* (thanking God for who he is). We have also thought through four hindrances to gratitude and specific biblical truths to help us overcome them. Yet as we seek to live our lives with a daily attitude of gratitude, let us now take a step further. Let us consider how we intentionally seek to not only thank the Lord for those gorgeous flowers in our lives but to thank him for thorns as well.

This may seem foolish at first glance. Does the Lord truly expect us to thank him for the hindrances? Whether it is a wayward child's rejection of God, cancer, depression, disability, guilt from the past, or a host of other things—how could we be thankful with any sincerity?

It is a joy to keep a blessing journal. We can gladly pray through it and be encouraged as we remember even a fraction of what the Lord has done for us. But is it biblical to keep a kind of "thorn list" for which we also seek to be thankful? Let's look back to Paul's words about his unnamed thorn:

> But [the Lord] said to me, "My grace is sufficient for you, for my power is made perfect in weakness." Therefore I will boast all the more gladly of my weaknesses, so that the power of Christ may rest upon me ... For when I am weak, then I am strong.
> 2 CORINTHIANS 12:9-10

Yes, this is the same thorn we read about in chapter 5 (page 76)—the thorn Paul asked the Lord three times to remove. And yes, Paul comes to a point where he is content with it. Yet his contentment and even boasting of it show Paul's understanding that the weakness the thorn produces is used by the Lord to show his power. He gives us strength when we feel weak. He is accomplishing his purposes in ways that our minds cannot understand. He will be glorified— and he is always working all things for our good (Romans 8:28).

Pearls of Wisdom from a Blind Man

Perhaps you are familiar with the classic hymn *O Love That Wilt Not Let Me Go*. It was written in 1882 by the blind Scottish minister and hymn-writer George Matheson.

1. *O Love that wilt not let me go,*
   I rest my weary soul in thee;
   I give thee back the life I owe,
   That in thine ocean depths its flow
   May richer, fuller be.

2. *O Light that followest all my way,*
   I yield my flickering torch to thee;
   My heart restores its borrowed ray,
   That in thy sunshine's blaze its day
   May brighter, fairer be.

3. *O Joy that seekest me through pain,*
   I cannot close my heart to thee;
   I trace the rainbow through the rain,
   And feel the promise is not vain,
   That morn shall tearless be.

4. *O Cross that liftest up my head,*
   I dare not ask to fly from thee;
   I lay in dust life's glory dead,
   And from the ground there blossoms red
   Life that shall endless be.

Struck with blindness at the age of 20, Matheson could certainly speak of thorns. He had been engaged, but when his fiancée learned he was going blind, she broke it off. His sister had been caring for him until she married. He wrote the hymn the day she married, and said he did so in just five minutes with no revisions. He never married and died of a stroke aged 64.

The hymn is a powerful reminder of our Lord's relentless love for us. I deeply appreciate Matheson's heartfelt words in this paraphrase of a prayer attributed to him:

> *My God, I have never thanked thee for my thorns. I have thanked thee a thousand times for my roses, but never once for my thorns. Teach me the glory of the cross I bear; teach me the value of my thorns. Show me that I have climbed closer to thee along the path of pain. Show me that, through my tears, the colors of your rainbow look much more brilliant.*[12]

How stunning it is for a blind man to speak of the brilliant colors of the rainbow! Oh that we would learn to thank the Lord for our suffering in specific ways as Matheson did. He asked the Lord to teach him four things: the glory of the cross he bore, the value of the thorns, the closeness to the Lord they brought him, and the brilliance of the Lord in the process. Perhaps this would be a good exercise for us as we test our sincerity to grow in gratitude.

Let's Try It Out

Join me in thinking about your sharpest thorn at present. Mine seems to occupy my mind more than I would care to admit. Satan desperately wants to use thorns to discourage and defeat us. How can we begin to think about bearing them as a cross that we would describe as glorious?

Since we do not live on desert islands, we can assume that other people in our lives are observing us as we bear the burden. Could it be that the Lord is orchestrating specific circumstances unknown to us to draw people to himself? Perhaps some of those observers will one day face similar circumstances, and the Lord is preparing them as they watch us. In some cases, we will be able to comfort them from our own experiences. No pressure! Paul makes this plain:

> *Blessed be the God and Father of our Lord Jesus Christ, the Father of mercies and God of all comfort,*

> *who comforts us in all our affliction, so that we may*
> *be able to comfort those who are in any affliction, with*
> *the comfort with which we ourselves are comforted by*
> *God.*   2 CORINTHIANS 1:3-4

When we get to heaven, it will be glorious to see how the Lord chose to use the way we bore our suffering to encourage others—even though those ways are at present completely lost on us.

Placing Worth on What Seems Worthless

Second, what can we say about the value of the thorns? We may see them as worthless distractions that too often get us sidetracked and, if we are not careful, can even define who we are. How is there any value in that? The answer goes to the absolute sovereignty of God. He is good. He is kind. He loves us. He is God and we are not.

A helpful saying, often attributed to Charles Spurgeon, summarizes this so well:

> *God is too good to be unkind and he is too wise to be*
> *mistaken. And when we cannot trace his hand, we*
> *must trust his heart. ... The sweetest prayers God ever*
> *hears are the groans and sighs of those who have no*
> *hope in anything but his love.*

This leads us to believe there must be a value in the thorn because, otherwise, God would not allow it to exist. He makes no mistakes. He is never mean-spirited or unkind. He sent his only Son to purchase our redemption. We are his! So, as Spurgeon wisely said, we go with that. We trust the heart of our all-knowing, all-loving, all-powerful God even when we don't understand his purposes. We must trust him and keep praying, even with groans.

Even in the Valley, God Is Good

Third, Matheson said he climbed closer to the Lord along the path of pain. We can hopefully all see this to be the case as we each consider our stickiest thorn. If we had no suffering in this life, we would be tempted to be self-sufficient. We would be grateful for our lives of ease, but we would never need to call upon the Lord. We would never know that he is indeed "our refuge and strength, a very present help in trouble" (Psalm 46:1).

It would be something like having the world's best fire extinguisher but never encountering a fire. While being thankful, we would never know, and might always wonder, if the super-duper extinguisher worked or not.

No one wishes for a fire—and no one asks for a thorn. But as believers who all have suffering of some kind, as Scripture says we will, we certainly take joy in knowing the Lord is true to his word. We cherish the closeness we feel to our Lord as we bear adversity. He truly is with us on the mountain tops and in the valleys. He is faithful! We can thus thank the Lord for the thorn as it is used to draw us near to the One who loves us more than we can ever imagine. It does have value after all.

Look for the Rainbow

Lastly, Matheson speaks of how the rainbow looks more brilliant though his tears. We know our suffering is temporary, but some days, it is hard to put that into perspective. Peter tells us that it is for "a little while." He goes on to remind us that we all suffer, but one day that will end by the hand of God himself:

> *And after you have suffered a little while, the God of all grace, who has called you to his eternal glory in Christ, will himself restore, confirm, strengthen, and establish you.* 1 PETER 5:10

I love this verse. So much theology coupled with hope is compacted here.

Meditate on it. Memorize it. You can anticipate that glorious rainbow when you do!

Dear reader, if you are experiencing tremendous suffering that is hard to even put into words, I wish I could sit beside you right now. The idea of thanking God when it hurts may at first strike you as insulting. Please know that I do not mean to minimize the seriousness of your circumstances in any way.

Do you often think about how we will spend eternity in the new creation with our risen Savior? It is a place where there will be no more dying, no more pain, no more diseases, no more tears, and no more separation from the Lord (Revelation 21:3-4). In the presence of our King, the blind will see, the deaf will hear, the mute will speak, the lame will walk, the mentally impaired will understand, and we will be with Jesus for ever and ever. How glorious!

Ten Ways to Thank God When It Hurts

In the meantime, we are called to make every day count as we walk on this earth. As we eagerly thank God for who he is and what he has done to bountifully bless us, we also must work on eagerly and specifically thanking him for trials.

Think through these ten specific ways with me and meditate on the accompanying Scriptures. We have covered a couple of these in this chapter already but they are included here all in one place.

- **Thank the Lord** for the resolve he has given you to not let your thorn in the flesh be the hallmark of your life. Ask him to help you boldly accept the good and the bad. *Shall we receive good from God, and shall we not receive evil?* (Job 2:10)

- **Thank the Lord** because he chose you to walk through this particular adversity for a particular reason. You may or may not know the reason this side of heaven but you can trust beyond a shadow of a doubt that there is one. *For who has known the mind of the Lord, or who has been his counselor?* (Romans 11:34)

- **Thank the Lord** because, whether you escape or endure this present affliction, your life is forever hidden with Christ in God. He will not leave you or forsake you. *For you have died, and your life is hidden with Christ in God.* (Colossians 3:3)

- **Thank the Lord** because, if you have shared your feelings, his children have likely shown his love to you in the process of your grief. You would not have felt that intense brotherly affection without the grief. *Love one another with brotherly affection. Outdo one another in showing honor.* (Romans 12:10)

- **Thank the Lord** because he can use your reaction to suffering to encourage struggling believers who observe you and who persevere in their own trials as a result. *And we urge you, brothers, admonish the idle, encourage the fainthearted, help the weak, be patient with them all.* (1 Thessalonians 5:14)

- **Thank the Lord** because he can use your response to suffering to encourage unbelievers and point them to Christ. They will see that your love for Christ is not dependent on being free from trials, but that you truly serve a God who is love at all times. *But thanks be to God, who in Christ always leads us in triumphal procession, and through us spreads the fragrance of the knowledge of him everywhere. For we are the aroma of Christ to God among those who are being saved and among those who are perishing.* (2 Corinthians 2:14-15)

- **Thank the Lord** because, whatever the burden is, he is going to teach you an important lesson in the process that you would not have otherwise learned. He will use it to make you more like Christ. *For this light momentary affliction is preparing for us an eternal weight of glory beyond all comparison.* (2 Corinthians 4:17)

- **Thank the Lord** because the particular thorn you bear will not overwhelm you. Your loving God knows exactly what you are able to bear. *No temptation has overtaken you that is not common to man. God is faithful, and he will not let you be tempted beyond your ability, but with the temptation he will also provide the way of escape, that you may be able to endure it.* (1 Corinthians 10:13)

- **Thank the Lord** for the dependence your grief causes you to have on him. It destroys any thought of self-reliance. And no one else can comfort you as he can. His loving care is perfect. *I have set the Lord always before me; because he is at my right hand, I shall not be shaken.*

Therefore my heart is glad, and my whole being rejoices; my flesh also dwells secure. (Psalm 16:8-9)

• **Thank the Lord** because you can anticipate the joy of being free from your suffering when you join him in heaven forever. Your pain will become a distant memory in the presence of our Lord. *You make known to me the path of life; in your presence there is fullness of joy; at your right hand are pleasures forevermore.* (Psalm 16:11)

These ten ways will help us thank God when it hurts. They will help us focus on him more than on our pain. They will help us trust in his goodness as we thank him for the thorns.

Dear Father,

We admit we would sooner praise you for the good things you give us than thank you for the trials. Please give us wisdom to do both.

May you make the roses in our lives smell even sweeter as we thank you for the thorns.

May you kindly allow us to see even a flash of what you are doing through our adversity but if not, may we still trust in you relentlessly.

Oh, come quickly, Lord Jesus!

Amen.

Think It Through

1. What do you think about starting a "thorn list" next to your "praise list"? Can you get excited about the possibility of the Lord showing you specific blessings that come as a result of thorns?

2. Look again at the "Ten Ways to Thank God When It Hurts." Is there an item from the list that jumps out at you? Stop now and pray the accompanying Scripture to the Lord, and ask him to give you fresh insight into your hurt.

Let's Do It!

Let's get practical in this final chapter as we think about ways to practice gratitude from a Christian worldview. First, we will build a framework to show how our thankfulness is based on our love for the Lord. Then, we will work through a list of several areas where gratitude can be a blessing to others.

Attitudes Trace to Ancient History

People who do not love Jesus certainly talk and write about gratitude. Some of the most gracious people you know may be unbelievers who intentionally find ways to show appreciation. But their basis for doing so is not grounded in thankfulness for the Lord's kindnesses. We are glad to receive gratitude from all, but realize it is not necessarily the norm for unbelievers—and this goes back for centuries. The ancient Roman philosopher, Tacitus, is quoted as saying:

Men are more ready to repay an injury than a benefit because gratitude is a burden and revenge is a pleasure.

Do you think this is true? By human nature, do we take pleasure in getting even for a perceived wrong? Do we view showing gratitude as a burden? When we watch many people on the street, we can see it's true even in simple things. If you cut in front of someone in traffic, you can be almost certain you will hear the sound of the horn or see an angry gesture. But if you hold the door open for someone, or allow a car to change lanes ahead of you, it is not at all certain that your kindness will be acknowledged.

As Christians, we do not want to view gratitude as a burden. We seek to gladly model it as a genuine act of caring for our fellow humans. We may appear to have the same motivation as the courteous atheist who thanks us when we hold the elevator door for her. Both of us are grateful for the act of kindness. But Christians are different in that we have a mindset of God's graciousness to us in all things. The Bible tells us to:

Let your reasonableness be known to everyone. The Lord is at hand. PHILIPPIANS 4:5

Our motivation is to overflow with thankfulness to the Lord and to let that spill over in the way we treat others. We desire to spend our days obeying Scripture as we love our neighbors as ourselves (Mark 12:31). That love includes joyfully expressing thanks—and leaving any revenge to the Lord (Romans 12:19).

The World's Observations

I was amused by this sign in a gift store:

> *Be pretty if you can; be witty if you must; be gracious if it kills you.*
> ELSIE DE WOLFE

This explains why outer beauty and great personality pale when accompanied by rudeness and ingratitude. Multiple studies now suggest that people who feel gratitude are more likely to have higher levels of happiness, and lower levels of depression and stress. *The New York Times* recently ran a feature story asserting that gratitude may even have health benefits.[13] Sure, unbelievers can be grateful to each other but it ends there. As the English writer G.K. Chesterton quipped:

> *The worst moment for an atheist is when he is really thankful and has no one to thank.*[14]

The best they can muster is something like "Thanks, Universe." I have even heard of some who say we must praise *ourselves* for how well we meet our own needs.

Nonsense! How blessed we are to call upon the name of the Lord with assurance that he wants to hear from us. Yes, the Creator of the universe is known to us. He is not an impersonal being but a loving God, whom we can call *Abba*, meaning Daddy (Romans 8:15)! Let's take this framework as we now consider how to show gratitude to others.

Gratitude Starts at Home: A Word to Married Women

Our first priority should be meeting the needs of those whom the Lord has given us in our families. How bizarre it would be if we were concerned about thanking friends and even strangers for kindnesses but we failed to show consistent gratitude to our families. Sadly, we can sometimes speak to loved ones in ways that we would never speak to strangers. May we be mindful of correcting this.

If you are married, you may wrongly assume that your husband already knows that you appreciate all he does as the servant leader in the home. You have told him that a few times so surely he knows, right? You may be surprised.

I have been blessed for over 30 years to be married to a very gifted Christian leader. People all over the world tell him how much his writing and speaking points them to Christ. He also receives more than his share of harsh criticism from those who do not agree with him. Yet no one is more proud of him than I am. I must not allow myself to falsely believe that the affirmation he receives from others is sufficient. He needs to know from me that I am grateful for who he is and for the sacrifices he makes daily for our family. I am thankful for his love and fidelity. I need to express that more often than in an occasional greeting card. It is important I express gratitude to him in front of our children as well as in front of his peers.

All of us who are married must seek to be more intentional about this. The Lord has blessed us with the gift of marriage. Yet we often find it easier to complain about what we do not appreciate than to be grateful for what we do.

My favorite quote from Elisabeth Elliot, missionary, author, and speaker, sums that up well:

> *It is always possible to be thankful for what is given rather than to complain about what is not given. One or the other becomes a habit of life ... Accept, positively and actively, what is given to you. Let thanksgiving be the habit of your life.*[15]

Courtesy Is an Expression of Gratitude

Have you noticed how "please" and "thank you" have somehow vanished as people tend to either grunt or say nothing at all? What about us? Do we always try to make eye contact with waitstaff, clerks, and bus drivers as we address them with common courtesy? Failure to do so is a lack of gratitude for a simple service rendered.

Courtesy is an expression of gratitude in its most basic form. This does not mean we walk around with cheesy smiles all of the time. Yet when we have gracious gratitude for the Lord in our hearts, it wells up and spills out toward others in a genuine way. And it's biblical:

> *Love one another with brotherly affection. Outdo one another in showing honor.* ROMANS 12:10

It is right and honorable to express gratitude for those who have made sacrifices for the service of your country. I encourage you to find a way to do that when you see men and women in uniform. They do not tire of being thanked for their service. It can be as simple as saying, "Thank you so much for serving us and our country so well." It can look much like encouragement.

How we cherish those whom the Lord has placed in our lives who seem to always have a word of encouragement for us just when we need it. Let's encourage loved ones as well as teachers, co-workers, neighbors, and friends. Let's show them we don't take them for granted, and express heartfelt thanks for things big and small. Unbelievers should see our efforts in this area as consistent with our actions to point them to Christ.

Let's Teach Our Children to Be Thankful

Krazy Straws, twisted into funny shapes, were all the rage when I was a child. I laughed out loud when I read this quip on Twitter:

One good thing about five-year-olds is that they are always just a Krazy Straw and some chocolate milk away from the best day ever.

It's so true! Life can be full of awe for five-year-olds. Innocent and free from the cares of this world, young children delight us by how easily they enjoy simple pleasures. They respond with glee that makes us want to bottle up their contentment forever.

But time marches on and life gets complicated. Those former five-year-olds grow up. Sadly, we see a sense of entitlement creep into the thought-processes of many adolescents. Too many of them suffer under the illusion that all good things are owed to them. They lack gratitude for the gift of the things they have. *Krazy Straws* become a distant memory.

Teaching children manners includes teaching them to express gratitude. We don't teach them manners so that they can be good little rule-keepers. We teach them about matters of the heart as we seek to show them God's character. But our teaching is empty if we do not model it for them. Children should routinely see us thanking others all day long. Neglecting this will produce children who have an entitlement mentality.

It is discouraging to watch teenagers who think they deserve things just because they are available—and because their peers have them. Too many parents go into debt to provide well beyond what is necessary because they give in to the pressure of wanting their kids to like them. Parents then seem surprised when their kids respond with an "it's about time" attitude and lack all gratitude. Some teenagers think they are entitled to all the good things life has to offer. If we don't get a handle on that quickly, it will spread like wildfire.

Let's teach children from an early age that every gift comes from the Lord (James 1:17). Help them understand that they should express thanks to the Lord first and foremost but they should also express thanks to family and friends. Habits formed will take root. Entitlement and self-absorption will be stifled. As proof of this, consider some adults you know who rarely seem to express thanks. It is likely they are not even aware of their attitude as it is a way of life. It is not too late to learn!

The Ministry of Written Thanks

While we are on the subject of being practical in our gratitude toward others, what about thanks expressed in writing? Many in our modern society have concluded that thank-you notes are simply old-fashioned and unnecessary. I once had a student who told me how she was conflicted about this. She was overwhelmed by the generous wedding gifts she and her husband received and wanted to write notes to express gratitude. But her husband insisted this would be a waste of time and money. They had registered for the gifts, so the givers already knew that they liked the purchased items. Why should they write notes to convince them, he reasoned?

He missed the point entirely. The givers were under no obligation to purchase anything for this couple. They were not *entitled* to what they listed on a registry. It was an act of kindness for the giver to spend time and money in the presentation of a gift of any kind. The wife was entirely right in wanting to send a thankful response. Ditto for any gift, home-cooked meal, provision of a guest room, or a host of other thoughtful gestures. Let's aspire to be people who encourage others with our gratitude.

I believe there is a right and a wrong way to write a thank-you note. Have you ever received one that appears to merely discharge the obligation? Sadly, they sometimes read like form letters:

> *Thanks for the gift. Thanks for sharing the day with us.*

While this is better than no note at all, it would be so much nicer to receive a note that states what the gift was and includes a sentence that is personal. For example:

> *It was thoughtful of you to choose a beautiful bowl that matches the color of our kitchen, and it is just the right size to serve many favorite recipes. Thank you.*

Sincere gratitude is a gift in itself. It is not difficult to learn this art.

Make Someone's Day

What a joy it is to go to the mail box and find a kind note! There is something about a handwritten note that trumps a text or an email. One day, we received a two-page handwritten note from the grown child of friends. The letter gave specific examples of how we had encouraged him over the years. There was no hidden agenda, such as a request for passing on his résumé. There was no favor needed as the letter drew to a close. It was simply an unexpected and very welcome expression of true gratitude from a young man who wanted us to know how thankful he is.

Let's cultivate the art of writing a note to someone in order to show gratitude and encouragement. If the Lord brings specific people to mind for no apparent reason, a short note written to simply say you thought of them and are thankful for what they mean to you could be used by the Lord in ways we vastly underestimate. We can certainly bless others with a text or an email, but I fear that we are losing the personal touch as we live with our smartphones in our hands. An actual phone call or a handwritten note carries more weight.

I have heard sweet stories of notes found tucked away in the Bibles of dear departed saints as family members sort through what is left behind. The notes had been written to the owners of the Bibles, sometimes many years before they died, but kept safely ever since. The writers of those notes are sometimes told about this and do not even remember writing the note.

But it meant enough to the recipient to keep it for years and presumably to read it over and over again as an encouragement. How blessed would you be to know that you were the writer of notes such as these?

Gratitude toward others shows both the presence of humility and the absence of entitlement. Let's keep looking for practical ways to express it to God's glory. Let's prove Tacitus wrong and never view it as a burden.

> *Father in heaven,*
>
> *We have been given your undeserved favor in ways we cannot begin to count.*
>
> *Please give us thankful hearts.*
>
> *Make us the kind of people who seek to outdo each other in showing gratitude, in the hope of encouraging others and pointing them to Christ.*
>
> *Thank you, Father. Amen.*

Think It Through

1. Are you intentional about making eye contact with people and using common courtesy on a daily basis? Do you agree that graciousness, or the lack of it, speaks volumes?

2. What's your practice of expressing thanks in writing? Do you send heartfelt thanks, form-letter thanks, or no thanks at all? How can this simple practice, done well, have ripple effects in encouraging others?

Conclusion: Gratitude That Honors The Lord

The wonderful summer season is now in full swing. It's much different from the crisp autumn days described at the beginning of this book. Long carefree days and stunning sunsets mark this happy season. Whether it is summer, autumn, winter, or spring, our Creator gives us great cause for gratitude in every season of the year.

But let us be honest: some believers are rarely thankful and perpetually cranky! They are so quick to be offended. When you jostle them, anything but gratitude spills out. And if truth be told, sometimes those believers are *us*. On the other hand, we all know believers who have walked through rough circumstances for much of their lives, yet when asked how they are faring, they say with a smile, "I'm better than I deserve!"

Which of those believers knows more joy? Which displays Christ? Which glorifies God? We may find developing an attitude of gratitude hard to do, but we can surely see that it is a wonderfully attractive way to live.

Why is it that some believers are more thankful than others? Is there a gratitude gene out there? Did some parents nail this life-lesson better than others with their kids? Or are some personalities just more like A.A. Milne's Eeyore than others? (Though Eeyore himself would most certainly encourage us to show gratitude, as he makes clear in *Winnie-the-Pooh* when he says, "A little Consideration, a little Thought for Others, makes all the difference."[16])

No, to all of the above. While it is certainly important for parents to both model and teach the importance of thankfulness, children will eventually decide for themselves whether they value this teaching or not. People with a joyful outlook will find it easier to be grateful, but thankfulness is a choice made by each of us moment by moment. We can choose to be thankful or we can choose to complain. Remember the earlier Elisabeth Elliot quote—"one or the other becomes a habit of life" (page 119). What a tragedy when we stop being blown away by the fact that there is a God in heaven who is perfect in every way. *And he knows our names!*

As we work through the obstacles discussed in the previous chapters, our goal is to *grow* in gratitude. We will never fully achieve perfect thankfulness on this side of heaven, but, by God's grace, let's pray to see progress. We seek to rediscover the joy of our salvation both when things are going our way and when they are not. It's not rocket science. And people are watching.

Thankfulness from the Core of Our Being

We must redeem the time! The Lord numbers our days and gives each one of us a specific little corner of the world to influence. How vital it is for us to wisely pour into others while we can. One of the great truths we can both model and teach is a life filled with thankfulness—and one clearly not marked by complaining. This is not a check-the-box lesson, but rather, thankfulness sprouts from the core of our being. It is genuine, heartfelt, irrepressible, and deepening. We do not arrive at an acceptable level of gratitude and call it a day. As we grow in maturity in the grace and knowledge of our Lord Jesus, we will discover new reasons to praise him even as we find new ways to thank him for characteristics he has held since eternity past.

So, gratitude really is a big deal. G. K. Chesterton put it this way:

> *I would maintain that thanks are the highest form of thought, and that gratitude is happiness doubled by wonder.*[17]

Let that sink in! He asserts there is no higher form of thought than thankfulness. I am not sure all scholars would agree. And many people on the street would dismiss thankfulness as a simplistic practice and not "the highest form of thought." But we know better. We have the immeasurable blessing of God's written word to us. We've seen that it tells us over and over and over again to be thankful (Psalm 95:2; Psalm

86:12; 1 Thessalonians 5:18). We are instructed to give thanks so many times because it does not come naturally to us in our sinful natures. Paul makes that plain in this prayer from Colossians, where he asks the Lord to make his readers thankful:

[May you be] strengthened with all power, according to his glorious might, for all endurance and patience with joy, giving thanks to the Father, who has qualified you to share in the inheritance of the saints in light.

COLOSSIANS 1:11-12

And don't you love the idea that gratitude is "happiness doubled by wonder"? We can apply that in both earthly and heavenly ways. I feel such happiness when I look into the face of my precious grandson. I am filled with joy by his presence, but I simultaneously feel a sense of profound wonder for who he is—the baby of my baby! How kind of the Lord to allow my husband and me to delight in this little boy and to see our dear daughter and son-in-law love him so well. I clearly see what Chesterton means by gratitude in that earthly sense.

A Savior To Thank Forever

Yet when I think about who my Savior is and how he rescued me, a sinner unable to save myself, I am overcome with happiness doubled by wonder in a heavenly sense. Words cannot come close to expressing that kind of gratitude. How awesome that we will get to spend eternity praising our great God (Psalm 52:9)!

We end where we began, with a clear command of Scripture, from the inspired pen of Paul:

> *Therefore, as you received Christ Jesus the Lord,*
> *so walk in him, rooted and built up in him*
> *and established in the faith, just as you were taught,*
> *abounding in thanksgiving.*   COLOSSIANS 2:6-7

That's our job in a nutshell! We received Christ Jesus the Lord. So let's walk in him and abound in thanksgiving as we do.

James Montgomery Boice was such a wise pastor. He died in 2000 at the age of 62 but left us many treasures in his writings. This is one of my favorite Boice quotes:

> *What we need today is not ever increasingly clever*
> *methods, still less increasingly clever people, but*
> *obedience informed and motivated by the living and*
> *abiding word of God.*[18]

Do you ever think of what would happen if Christians would just be obedient? How glorious would it be if we played by the rules using that "living and abiding word" (1 Peter 1:23)? Let's rediscover the joy of thankfulness. Let's grow in gratitude with each passing day. Our God deserves our highest praise from our whole hearts.

Endnotes

Chapter 1

1 Albert Mohler, *They Did Not Honor Him or Give Thanks—Why Thanksgiving is Inescapably Theological,* http://www.albertmohler.com/2015/11/23/they-did-not-honor-him-or-give-thanks-why-thanksgiving-is-inescapably-theological/

Chapter 2

2 Jonathan Edwards, *The Works of Jonathan Edwards, Vol. 17: Sermons and Discourses, 1730-1733.*

3 John Piper, *A Godward Life* (Multnomah, 1997), p 213-214.

4 Chuck Colson, *Radical Gratitude: Grateful to God in Tough Times,* http://www.breakpoint.org/2011/06/breakpoint-radical-gratitude/

Chapter 3

5 Charles Bridges, *The General Causes of Want of Success in the Christian Ministry,* http://graceonlinelibrary.org/church-ministry/pastoral-ministry/the-general-causes-of-want-of-success-in-the-christian-ministry-by-charles-bridges/

6 John Piper, Plenary Address: "True Woman," October 9, 2008.

Chapter 4

7 Kevin DeYoung, *Crazy Busy*, (IVP USA, 2013), p 118.

8 Paul E. Miller, *A Praying Life*, (NavPress, 2009), p 23.

Chapter 5

9 http://equip.sbts.edu/audio/student-life-conference-life-lessons-disability-ministry-session-1/

10 http://equip.sbts.edu/chapel/2-corinthians-121-10/

Chapter 6

11 Chris Castaldo, https://www.thegospelcoalition.org/article/the-remedy-to-religious-guilt, August 1, 2013.

Chapter 7

12 Quoted in *Our Daily Bread,* https://odb.org/2001/09/16/thanks-for-thorns/

Chapter 8

13 https://www.nytimes.com/2017/03/27/well/live/positive-thinking-may-improve-health-and-extend-life.html

14 G.K. Chesterton, *St. Francis of Assisi,* (1923), p 88.

15 Elisabeth Eliot, *Love Has a Price Tag,* (Vine Books, 1990), p 97.

Conclusion

16 A.A. Milne, *Winnie-the Pooh*

17 G.K. Chesterton, From "Christmas and Salesmanship," a short essay published in 1935.

18 James Montgomery Boice. *Come to the Waters,* (Baker Books, 2011), p 51.

Thank You

I am indebted to several groups of people as I step out with this first published work.

My family—including my dearest husband, Al; our precious children, Christopher Mohler, and Katie and Riley Barnes; and my beloved mother, Mary Kahler—have all encouraged me in their own sweet ways throughout the writing process.

My loyal friends have also served as cheerleaders, asking good questions and praying for me faithfully. Thank you, Jodi, Selwyn, and Harriet!

My students in Seminary Wives Institute at Southern Seminary have inspired me for twenty years now and continue to do so.

My editor, Alison Mitchell, has been nothing short of stellar as she has patiently worked with me in all phases of *Growing in Gratitude*. After hearing me speak on gratitude, she surprised me by insisting that there was a book to be drawn from my material. Thank you, Alison, for your keen insight and cheerful assistance.

To God be all the glory!

Suffering is real. But so is hope.

This is a book for those who are going through a time of struggle, or who love someone who is. A book for women who feel perplexed, defeated, struck down, abandoned, or despairing. A book written by two women who are walking through these times themselves. A book that gives hope—because God wants to give us hope, not just beyond our hurts but in our hurts.

Hard questions. Beautiful truth.

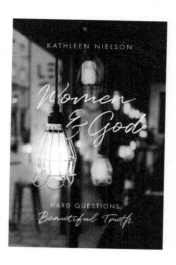

Is God sexist? In this warm, conversational, sympathetic book, Kathleen Nielson looks at what the Bible really says about women. She asks the hard questions on this most emotive subject, showing how truth can not just be believed but enjoyed. Women of all backgrounds, views, and ages will find this a valuable book. Also ideal for use in women's ministry.

thegoodbook.com/women-and-god
thegoodbook.co.uk/women-and-god

Depression, anxiety, and the difference Jesus makes

Whether you have experienced mental illness yourself or want to understand depression and anxiety to care for somebody you love, this book provides a personal and theologically thoughtful reflection on the challenges facing Christians in this area.

thegoodbook
COMPANY

BIBLICAL | RELEVANT | ACCESSIBLE

At The Good Book Company, we are dedicated to helping Christians and local churches grow. We believe that God's growth process always starts with hearing clearly what he has said to us through his timeless word—the Bible.

Ever since we opened our doors in 1991, we have been striving to produce resources that honor God in the way the Bible is used. We have grown to become an international provider of user-friendly resources to the Christian community, with believers of all backgrounds and denominations using our Bible studies, books, evangelistic resources, DVD-based courses, and training events.

We want to equip ordinary Christians to live for Christ day by day, and churches to grow in their knowledge of God, their love for one another, and the effectiveness of their outreach.

Call us for a discussion of your needs or visit one of our local websites for more information on the resources and services we provide.

Your friends at The Good Book Company

NORTH AMERICA
UK & EUROPE
AUSTRALIA
NEW ZEALAND

thegoodbook.com
thegoodbook.co.uk
thegoodbook.com.au
thegoodbook.co.nz

866 244 2165
0333 123 0880
(02) 9564 3555
(+64) 3 343 2463

WWW.CHRISTIANITYEXPLORED.ORG
Our partner site is a great place for those exploring the Christian faith, with a clear explanation of the good news, powerful testimonies and answers to difficult questions.